WILLIAM AND MARY

Mary Ede

Arts and Society in England
under
WILLIAM AND MARY

Mary Ede

STAINER AND BELL : LONDON

Printed and bound in Great Britain by Butler & Tanner Ltd, Frome and London

Production and design services by Elron Press Ltd, London WC2
Set in Monophoto Erhardt

ISBN 0 85249 480 7

Contents

FOR MY FAMILY

Author's Acknowledgements

This book makes no claim to be an original contribution to the art history of the period and I can only begin to express my debt to scholars in this field. Some of their names can be found in Appendix 2 but I should like to single out the stimulating writings of Dr Margaret Whinney and Dr Judith Hook. My interest in the period is long standing but only since my involvement with the Open University and its interdisciplinary approach have I been drawn into the absorbing field of arts and society. It has been a stimulating experience and I am grateful to friends and colleagues within the Arts Faculty. My debt to other people is great: to the staff of museums, libraries and galleries for their kindness; to owners and guardians who willingly showed me their treasures; to Patsy Lewis and Richard Butcher for their photographs and to Felicity Butcher for reading some of the draft chapters; and to my family who tolerated my temporary obsession with the 1690s and without whose encouragement I might never have finished the book. My elder son, Michael, in particular, helped with the index. But my greatest debt is to my husband whose patience and constant support, quite apart from his photographic role, makes this book as much his as mine.

English Society in 1688

The decade after the Glorious Revolution produced some notable works of art: Wren's design for Greenwich Hospital, Congreve's *Love for Love*, Purcell's *Dido and Aeneas*, the portrait of Dryden by Kneller. These are well known, and deservedly so. But at the other end of the scale there are many humbler examples: a Cotswold chest-tomb, a silver tankard, the woodcut on a broadsheet, the catchy tune of a ballad. All these must be included if we are trying to understand the relationship of English society at the end of the seventeenth century with the arts it produced. We are concerned here with what may be termed the artistic dimension of life. This embraces not only the aristocratic patronage of painters and architects but also the pargetting on an Essex house, or the traditional Morris dance. This wide definition of the arts has its difficulties. When does a bowl which is made as a container become a work of art? Is it only when the surface is beautifully decorated, or can the shape itself be considered? Or again, when does a building go beyond the criterion of function and become a work of architecture? And when, if ever, does a piece of woven cloth become an artistic hanging? In this blurred area of function and design the most helpful line seems to be that which divides bare necessity from some extra ingredient. This is usually embellishment, but can be concerned with form. A barn is built to store grain, and anything with walls, roof and door will serve the purpose. It becomes part of man's artistic creation when the combination of line and material produces visual pleasure. A burial place does not need to be marked by more than a plain headstone: it can become a work of art when the stone is carved and the lettering designed in a way that goes beyond the mere imparting of information. Of course this is an area wide open to subjective opinions, but I hope that this broader approach to the arts of the late seventeenth century will increase understanding of the society that produced them, and will also increase our enjoyment of the rich and varied heritage that survives.

But first we must consider what kind of society had developed in England by the late seventeenth century.

There were upwards of five and a half million people living in England and Wales in 1688 according to the contemporary Gregory King. His estimate, which is the first reasonably accurate one before the days of the national census, was based on careful surveys and examination of tax returns. Modern historians have found it reliable in those parts where independent checking has been possible and only minor adjustments have been suggested. At least three-quarters of the population still lived in rural surroundings in villages and hamlets, and even the market towns were tiny by modern standards, averaging little more than a thousand people. These, too, were dominated by agriculture, with regular markets in the distinctive squares or oblong areas that can still be seen in their hundreds today. Quite a number of their inhabitants were employed directly in farming, and others in trades that depended on agriculture. Land and the seasons ruled most people's lives.

Of the larger towns, probably only six outside London contained more than ten thousand people. Norwich, with thirty thousand, and Bristol, with twenty thousand were the largest; Newcastle, Exeter, York and Great Yarmouth came next. Below these were about twenty-four towns with populations estimated between five thousand and ten thousand. In the next rank Lichfield, a cathedral city and county centre, contained only two thousand, eight hundred and sixty-one people, as we know from a contemporary census. It would have been possible to walk round the walls of Bath, a city much the size of Lichfield, in fifteen minutes or reach the town fields from the centre in four or five[1]. It is difficult to describe the inhabitants of such places as urban-dwellers in any modern sense and yet contemporaries were well aware of the differences between rural and town society. The towns were markets and centres of communications. A town like Worcester had a normal market radius of about fifteen miles. Norwich, as a regional capital, sold cattle from Scotland to London dealers. Many towns were still walled, and this set them apart physically and symbolically from the country outside, even if their defensive purpose had been superseded. Even today we can sense the feeling of security and solidarity of the urban environment when we come suddenly into an old market town like Chipping Sodbury in Avon. Royal charters gave political and economic privileges and a variety of borough courts. Dif-

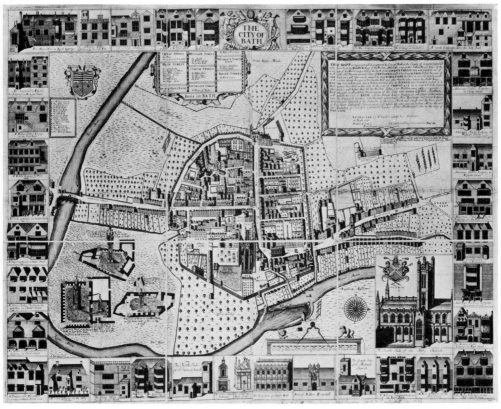

1. Bath in 1694

ferent towns in each county welcomed the justices at quarter sessions, and some the judges on assize. These were occasions for social gatherings and the enjoyment of balls, concerts and plays. Grammar schools offered the chance of an education beyond the reading, writing and arithmetic of the petty schools. None of this could be found in a village.

The urban population of the country was growing faster than the population as a whole, though this was not uniform, and London was perhaps growing fastest of all. The overall rate of population growth seems to have slowed down in the second half of the seventeenth century though there were local variations. On the one hand there is evidence from the Devon village of Colyton of a consistently higher number of burials than births during the greater part of the century; on the other hand areas like the Midlands and the Home Counties increased their population, but this may have been caused by newcomers taking advantage of expand-

11

ing industries like the Nottingham stocking industry or market gardening
in Kent or Middlesex. London was probably attracting at least eight thousand new arrivals each year (little, if any, of its rapid growth being due
to natural increase) and was a giant among the other English cities with

2. London in 1710, dominated by Wren's spires and St Paul's Cathedral

3. Shop signs in Cheapside, London

over half a million inhabitants. By 1700 it was the largest city in Europe.
But it was the only city in the British Isles that could stand comparison
with the great continental centres, and this tremendous difference in scale

between the capital and the next largest, Norwich, which was nearly twenty times smaller, needs to be emphasised. Ogg, the historian, has called London 'a microcosm of the nation' from the immense variety of life that could be found in the capital. It was the dominant centre of every aspect of the national life: commercial, political, social and cultural.

London's population had long since spilled over outside the city walls. By the end of the seventeenth century the land to the north of the Strand was built up as far as Great Russell Street and development had opened up the fashionable areas of Soho, St Giles's and St James's. The West End had come into being. To the east of the City was a mass of small houses, tenements and slums outside the control or concern of the City authorities. Most of the industries of the capital, spawned by the activities of the port, were concentrated here, accentuating the contrast with the opulent residential and pleasure-seeking West. Within the City itself,

4. William and Mary. Whitehall Palace and the Banqueting House in background

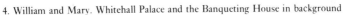

13

between the two Ends and rebuilt on the lines of the old street pattern after the Great Fire (though in brick and in a uniform style), was a concentration of merchant and business wealth that in its highest reaches equalled that of the nobility. But London was not only the commercial capital of England; it was also the social and cultural capital. Here were the headquarters of lawyers in the Inns of Court and in Westminster the seat of Parliament and the main royal courts of justice. The old Whitehall Palace in all its hotchpotch of buildings [see 4] still housed the Court and a miscellany of government offices and straddled the way beyond the Strand between the new fashionable areas and Westminster. A merchant M.P. for the City of London could easily reach the House of Commons, press for some office for an acquaintance in Whitehall, meet friends in a coffee house near St James's and so pass readily between the two cities of London and Westminster, contiguous but always distinct.

London's dominant position in the life of the nation has been a constant theme in English history but perhaps never more so than in the late seventeenth century before the momentum of the industrial revolution got under way. As communications improved, the centralising process accelerated, and the capital exercised a growing influence over the social, cultural and artistic fashions of the country. Not only did one in ten Englishmen live in London but it has been calculated that one adult in six in England had some direct experience of life in the capital. It is significant that the flood of immigrants came from all over England and though the poorer ones were unlikely to maintain any link with their previous areas, others kept contact with their families in the country. Hester Pinney, for example, was the unmarried daughter of a Puritan minister in Dorset ejected at the Restoration and she sold lace in London, first as part of the family business and then on her own account. Letters and occasional visits kept her in touch with the various members of the family. Similar links were probably maintained by apprentices in London and these traditional immigrants to the capital came from very far afield. Among those apprentices taking out the freedom of the City in 1690, for example, were eleven from Cumberland and six from Westmorland, and a few from Scotland, Ireland and the Channel Islands. Nearly three-quarters of the total of one thousand, five hundred and ninety apprentices for that year originated outside London and its immediate neighbourhood. We do not know how many of them may have become outward migrants and taken their skills and London-formed attitudes to provincial towns but Professor Glass has suggested that the net migration into London may easily hide much larger numbers of outward and inward migrants.

More significant, however, for the diffusion of London ideas and fashions was the succession of temporary visitors for educational, business or social reasons. Boys came up to London for schooling at Westminster under the great Dr Busby or in the smart academies springing up in the West End; young men studied at the Inns of Court. Business drew people of all ages and social standing, from a youth like Ralph Thoresby of Leeds, who spent a year or two learning his trade with a relative, to a corn chandler from Cambridgeshire or a merchant from Bristol. More and more families of the gentry expected to enjoy a few weeks in the capital, even if they could not afford the costs of a town establishment, and their friends in the country would commission them to bring back fashionable luxuries from the London shops. Litigation brought suitors and lawyers; Parliament, peers and members of the Commons. All these played their part in strengthening the influence of London over the rest of the country in the area of social custom, fashion and cultural attitudes, for the majority of visitors were people of standing in their own localities. The effects of this London dominance will be a recurring theme as the different arts are considered in detail.

Though some contemporaries thought London's expansion was a drain on the rest of the country, others saw its growth and that of other cities as a sign of national prosperity. Gregory King estimated that French average incomes were about twenty per cent below average incomes in England (and France was the greatest power in Europe with its twenty million people and its record of military success under Louis XIV), and that the Dutch average incomes were only slightly higher than the English. Since the Dutch had been England's commercial rivals throughout the century their wealth had been admired and envied and their trading practices copied. There seemed to observers an obvious connection between trade and national prosperity. So it is not surprising to find that overseas commerce dominates the economic literature of the time. Moreover, the evidence of expanding trade was there for everyone to see, particularly in London. More ships, and bigger ones, were being built. The East India Company was bringing home quantities of pepper and Indian and Chinese textiles; the colonies sent increasing amounts of sugar and tobacco. In the opposite direction went the traditional cloth exports, but different varieties of the 'new draperies' were now replacing the heavy broadcloth as demand for this lessened, and they were shipped direct to foreign ports, ranging from the Baltic to the eastern Mediterranean. Obvious, too, were the individual fortunes being made, for the wealthiest merchants still lived in the centre of London. The City had not yet taken on its modern character of daytime activity and nightly desertion. As a pressure group (or groups, for their interests often clashed) merchants were familiar in Westminster and were well represented in the Commons. They did in fact wield an influence greater than their numbers or economic power warranted. Two particular reasons for this may be mentioned here. The first is the part played by the merchant group in financing the Government's war expenditure. For, without the new methods of funding government borrowing through the Bank of England and associated channels of public credit, William III's campaigns would have been impossible (see p. 48). The second reason is the contemporary opinion already referred to, that England's prosperity came from her export trade and particularly from the export of woollen cloth.

While England's prosperity was more widely based than this – there was an increasing range of industries which were exploiting the resources of the country, and agriculture itself was still the mainspring of the economy – nevertheless the expansion of overseas trade in the second half of the seventeenth century was of crucial significance. The value of exports rose from £2½ million in 1660 to £4½ million by 1700, and most of this was achieved before the Revolution. Woollen cloth was still the largest single export in 1700 and had increased in value, but was no longer responsible for eighty per cent of the total exports as it had been in the middle of the century. The expansion had come in an entirely new area: the re-exporting to Europe of both Far Eastern goods and colonial sugar and tobacco. Under the protection of the Navigation Acts English ships had captured the giant's share of the carrying trade from the Dutch. The re-export trade in itself did not encourage further industries beyond shipping and the ancillary crafts connected with it, but the improvements in banking and credit management, and the lowering of interest rates all enabled a wider investment in economic ventures. The 1690s saw, for example, the first of the series of private Acts of Parliament for river improvements, turnpike acts and port development. New introductions included the manufacture of tin-plate, and these years saw a burst of inventions encouraged by the needs of war but following the line of practical investigation that had been launched by the Royal Society. Among these were Savery's patent for a steam pump in 1698 and Newcomen's application of the principle to an engine: heralds of a great technological future.

Who gained from this increasing prosperity? Did the rich get richer or was there any widespread benefit for the population? Lack of evidence makes certainty in the field impossible, but it seems likely that there was a slight improvement in the average standard of living. The second half of the seventeenth century saw not only a reduction in the rate of population growth but also an end to the long period of rising prices. The long-term trend in grain prices was in fact slightly downward, though periods of bad harvest caused temporary rises, as in the mid-1690s. Moreover, demand for labour pushed up wages slightly. But this minimal improvement must be seen against the very low standard of living of the mass of the people. King reckoned that over half the population were 'decreasing the wealth of the Kingdom' and included in this category labourers, cottagers, paupers and common seamen and soldiers. These lived on the edge of poverty, liable at some time to become destitute. Cottagers might be able to eke a living for themselves and their families in good years, but with no reserves a bad harvest or illness could spell starvation. Labourers on day wages faced under-employment if the weather was bad, and workers in any of the domestic or other industries had no guarantee of jobs if employers laid them off. Returns for a long day's work were in any case very small: twelve to sixteen pence for the unskilled labourers, eighteen to twenty-four pence for the craftsmen. The average yearly income for a wage-earner's family was only ten pounds. Above this subsistence level there was a great range of average incomes, according to King, from the forty-five pounds a year for the families of shopkeepers to the four hundred pounds for those of overseas merchants and over three thousand pounds for great landowners. Within these averages there were enormous variations in the incomes of individuals. Inequalities of wealth were the accepted marks of a hierarchical society in which the ruling minority was only a twentieth of the total population.

Status within this ruling segment was determined by title, but this was closely linked to wealth. At the peak of the social pyramid were about a hundred and sixty families of the nobility whose wealth came largely from great estates. Below them, again on King's figures, were eight hundred baronets, six hundred knights, three thousand esquires and twelve thousand gentlemen, all living chiefly from landed rents. The status of gentlemen was also accorded to perhaps another thirty-three thousand who were not living on estates in land but whose income was sufficient to free them from manual work: merchants, lawyers and other professionals, clergymen, army and navy officers. The crucial division in society came between those who were gentlemen and those who were not. The divisions above were far less important. The aristocracy were the leaders of society by virtue of their wealth and titles, but were not isolated from the gentry by any rigid class barriers. Nobles occupied the first rank in Parliament in the House of Lords, at Court and in the counties; the gentry below them were in the House of Commons and on the county commissions of the Peace. But they shared a common background and outlook.

This was a social hierarchy based on land, and despite the existence of other sources of wealth and other occupations progress up its ladder was most easily obtained by the acquisition of estates. Only in London was there anything approaching the urban patriciates of Amsterdam or Venice, and even here the wealthy merchants were closely allied with the landed gentry and frequently hailed from this group in the first place. Moreover, even the appearance of such 'urban' gentry did not lessen the powerful influence of the traditional leaders of society. Social emulation of the upper ranks ensured that the pattern of spending and social and cultural activities were closely modelled on that of the landowning class. There was a great deal of social mobility in the late seventeenth century, downwards as well as upwards, and it had a marked effect on the patronage of the arts since consumption in this area was an accepted way of expressing status. The economic conditions of the time enabled some exceptional fortunes to be made in trade, banking or government office, and their owners became very conspicuous spenders indeed. There was also a tendency towards the creation of some very large landed estates and a consequent increase in wealth available to some individuals for rebuilding or other expensive pursuits. The mere existence of surplus wealth cannot be equated with the patronage of the arts, and we need to look at the structure of such financial patronage to see in what ways the kind of society that existed in England at this time encouraged spending on the arts. However, we must also remember that the area of traditional custom, especially in dance and music, is largely unaffected by spending power. It can of course be influenced by economic changes. The enclosure of the open fields of a village could make the corporate celebrations less significant and any population movement made inroads on the traditional habits. With this exception, however, the arts depended on financial patronage.

Without question the most important source of such patronage was the Crown. The royal court was still organised at the end of the seventeenth century on the pattern of a household, though the needs of government had already outgrown this concept and administration was taking a more modern shape. Patronage of all kinds was exercised through the structure of household posts, and in the area of the arts there were such offices as Sergeant-Painter, Master Sculptor, Royal Gardener, and the post that Wren held for so long, that of Surveyor-General. Some were

5. Castle Howard, Yorkshire: the garden front by Vanbrugh

sinecures, some more onerous, but all were places that the Crown could bestow. The Stuarts had been discriminating patrons of the arts both in the appointments made within the royal household and in their personal collections and commissions. This tradition was maintained by William and Mary, but there were important changes after the Revolution. As we shall see later (see p. 46) the shift of power from Crown to Parliament was not just a political matter. There was an increasing separation of Household from government and more and more of the royal appointments were made by the king's government and not by the king. So aristocratic power increased through the manipulation of royal patronage. In social terms, however, the Court remained supreme arbiter of fashion. Royal tastes were copied avidly. The rush to imitate Queen Mary's passion for porcelain and delftware gave Defoe an opportunity to poke gentle fun at his countrymen. 'The Queen brought in the Custom

or Humour as I may call it of furnishing Houses with China-Ware . . .
piling their China upon the Tops of Cabinets, Scritoires and every Chimney-Piece, to the Tops of the Ceilings.' Status in late seventeenth-century
England was expressed by a man's style of living and there was social
pressure to compete in extravagant display. This did not always result
in a discerning patronage: some of its products were ornate without being
artistic. But there were several intelligent, knowledgeable and discriminating men among the aristocracy. Even by European standards Mon-
tague, Exeter and Shrewsbury were highly sensitive patrons.

It was only among members of the aristocracy (and a handful of commercial tycoons) that private individuals could be found who were
wealthy enough to patronise the arts on a grand scale. The list of the
great houses rebuilt in the 1690s is a reminder of their enormous wealth:
Petworth, Chatsworth[52], Burley-on-the-Hill, Castle Howard[5] are
only some of those palaces which represented a challenge to the Crown
in its dominance of artistic patronage.

Aristocratic patronage was exercised through the household in exactly
the same way as the Crown dispensed offices. Beyond the outlay on maintaining a large establishment in London as well as in the country and
the encouragement this could be to all kinds of craftsmen, a nobleman
like the Duke of Bedford expected to offer permanent employment to
musicians and artists. An Italian violoncello player and composer was
being paid a salary of one hundred guineas in 1702, and a second musician
was employed to help the Duke in collecting items for his music library.
Such aristocratic provision for the artist was a survival of the sixteenth-
century practice, but in a society where the artist had become largely independent so that the relationship was different. Such a servant in the aristocratic household had become a professional. His employer was much
more likely to treat him (if he became successful) as socially acceptable
and to see himself as the centre of an artistic or literary circle. Beyond
this there were other opportunities. Promising young men of letters might
be appointed tutors to sons making the Grand Tour or presented to liv-
ings within a nobleman's gift. Others might win his influence in obtaining
a government office or sinecure.

But the commonest form of aristocratic patronage was in individual
purchases and commissions. What was bought depended on a variety of
factors: the patron's personal interests, the agent he employed, the desire
to follow the latest fashion, a recommendation from relatives or friends.
In this respect aristocratic patronage was no different from that of the
less wealthy. It was, however, much more likely to result in the adoption

6. Elaborate furniture for display: japanned cabinet on gilt stand

of new styles. Those aristocrats who were close to the Court were more likely to be in touch with European fashions and, as social leaders, were followed by their inferiors. It was fortunate for the arts that conspicuous spending in this area was a symbol of status and, in particular, resulted in lavish housing and furnishings. New buildings were frequently undertaken where new wealth was suddenly acquired. Often they denoted the successful point of a social climber's career, perhaps the purchase of an estate by a wealthy merchant, financier or government official. Sometimes the new spender was the heir coming into his inheritance, or was the bridegroom of an heiress. Petworth was rebuilt after the marriage of the Percy heiress to the Duke of Somerset. Burley-on-the-Hill cost the second Earl of Nottingham thirty thousand pounds and was made possible by the income and perquisites of government office. There are plenty of examples of merchants or financiers setting themselves up in small landed estates and buying themselves position with a new house. The home counties was a favourite area, and a number of handsome houses of this date survive[58]. The amount of rebuilding in the late seventeenth century and into the early eighteenth supports the evidence for social mobility, but sometimes it is as much a lateral mobility as an upward. Many of such rising members of the business community were younger sons of landed families or the descendants of younger sons, and their movement back into the landed classes was an easy transition. John Helder, however, came from a humble freeholder's family in Gloucestershire, and the lovely group of brick farm buildings at Taynton was begun in the 1690s with his wife's dowry of one thousand pounds.

Beyond individual patronage seventeenth-century society encouraged certain corporate forms of patronage. The Crown ought to be considered under this heading as well, particularly when the financing of some of the royal projects is considered. The idea of Greenwich as a hospital for seamen had originally been put forward by James II, but nothing happened until Queen Mary took it up again after the victory of La Hogue. The design was Wren's (see p. 124 and ill. 7), and staff from the Office of Works were involved. But it was carried out by a Commission who were responsible for raising the money by public subscriptions, deductions from the seamen's pay and lottery tickets. John Evelyn was the treasurer, and the lack of funds hindered the progress of the building. William himself had promised two thousand pounds a year but owed eight thousand pounds by the time of his death, and there were other large sums outstanding. This method of entrusting major public works to a committee was not new: it had been used by Charles I and by his son for the rebuild-

7. Greenwich Hospital from the river

ing of London after the fire and for the new St Paul's. It was used again after 1710 for the fifty proposed new churches in London. Patronage by a group made many projects possible and involved more people in them, but committee decisions encouraged compromise and this acted as a brake on innovation. More than anyone else Wren suffered from the conflict of interests on such committees. He never had a free hand in any of his major works. His ability to adapt amounted to genius, and nowhere was it so triumphant as at Greenwich where he was forced to abandon his first scheme in order to keep the Queen's House as part of the plan.

City corporations offered another kind of group patronage. A new guildhall might be built or refurnished; presentation plate was often commissioned by an outgoing mayor. Regulations over building materials might encourage a new style, as at Warwick, with new brick houses to attract a better class of tenant. The London Companies had to rebuild their halls after 1666, and since refurnishing took many years there was considerable patronage of wood carvers, goldsmiths, painters and others. Dramatists were involved in the pageants for the Lord Mayor's Show and sign painters to decorate barges and floats (see p. 109). Institutions like the universities, the Inns of Court or the College of Physicians could be builders. Oxford and Cambridge both produced some notable additions to colleges at this time, and at Christ's Hospital there was a new Writing School (see p. 126). Institutions offered patronage, too, to painters for portraits of their office-holders, and at Oxford the University was forming an important collection of historical portraits. It is not surprising that such group patrons were urban. The only corporate patron that also functioned in the country was the Church. But even here there was a bias towards the town, at least in the proportion of the arts sponsored. Destruction by fire and the consequent need for rebuilding account mainly for this. St Paul's and the City churches in London are major examples in the 1690s (St Paul's was opened for worship in 1697 still without its dome or the western towers, and it was not until this decade that most of the interiors of the City churches were being tackled and some of the steeples built)[50, 51]. Another example is the parish church of St Mary's at Warwick which is an individual design in seventeenth-century Gothic of great interest. The Church of course did not exercise the kind of patronage it had enjoyed before the Reformation nor on such a scale. There was no room in an Anglican church for the statues or paintings that decorated a baroque interior of Catholic France or Italy. Though the Church of England maintained it was both Catholic and Protestant in its inheritance, it was the Puritan condemnation of ornament as superstitious trappings that prevailed in the matter of decoration. Bare whitewashed walls were the normal background to worship, and the nearest pictorial commission that a parish church would give was a decorative border to the Ten Commandments (like the one in Cameley, Somerset) or a new Royal Arms. Sculptors had the opportunity to design monuments, but these were private individual commissions from the dead person's family and not within the corporate patronage of the Church itself.

The distribution of wealth was the most fundamental of the economic factors influencing the arts. The greater the wealth, the greater the opportunity for artistic patronage. At the other end of the scale the fifty per cent of the population who were at near subsistence level had no choice but to spend their meagre income on necessities. Between the two extremes were many of the 'middling sort' who found that they were sharing in the increased prosperity of the country and were able to buy more and more of the semi-luxuries for their homes. So the yeoman who ordered a set of new chairs with their cane seats and high scrolled backs[71] and the prosperous brewer's wife who bought a delftware posset-cup[87] were both playing their part in the intricate network of patronage. They chose their purchases because they liked them and because they were fashionable. But they were also part of the wider economic network that made such goods available. The complex relationship between the whole field of the arts and the economic structure of the country can be illustrated by a brief look at some of the effects of overseas trade. Apart from the increased prosperity that expansion brought, the actual goods imported affected social habits and the forms of decoration. Coffee not only introduced a new drink but a new setting for its consumption. Coffee houses, which in London numbered two thousand by the reign of Anne and were already being copied in provincial cities, provided a forum for

8. Coffee house interior

the increasingly open society that was developing[8]. For though the coffee house was in one way a superior alternative to the tavern, a place for 'politer' society, it was far from being exclusive. Certain houses became the natural haunt of bankers or writers, but it was many years before any of them developed into a private club. So painter and merchant, lawyer and scrivener, writer, banker and country gentleman could all meet and talk. Out of it grew the new literary journalism that produced *The Spectator* in the next reign and the best method for the diffusion of upper-class fashions and ideas that could ever have been devised. Tea took longer to establish itself as a fashionable drink and was not widely drunk before 1700. But the East had already made an impact on the decoration of furniture and household goods. Chinoiserie designs were popular during Charles II's reign, and as the East India Company multiplied its trade at the end of the century it brought back larger quantities of textiles, japanned cabinets and china. These were copied by English craftsmen with varying degrees of accuracy[6, 9, 86, 87]. In particular

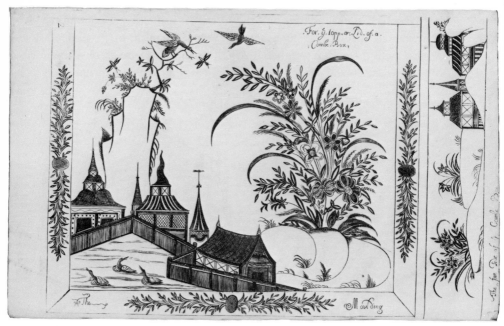

9. Design for a japanned box

this contact with the East increased the appetite for chinaware and the desire to find the secret of real porcelain; and though it was half a century before English experimenters were successful the impetus led to developments in stoneware (see p. 184).

External trade brought in new articles and new designs; the inland trade's influence on the arts was less direct but no less important. The general increase in the movement of goods about the country made certain manufactured articles, and therefore knowledge of current designs, more easily available. Cheaper processes encouraged a wider interest in the arts: engraving, for example, played an important part not only in spreading knowledge of pictorial art (see p. 115) but also in the rapid expansion of music publishing in the 1690s (see p. 84). In textiles the Norwich cloth industry produced a cheaper version of the printed patterned calicoes that were the fashionable luxury fabrics imported by the East India Company. In pottery, Lambeth and Bristol delftware[87] offered a decorative substitute for the real china that only the wealthy could afford.

It cannot be said that there was any real mass production of art in the sense of the nineteenth-century invention of photography or the pressing machine but cheaper lines were reaching more consumers and influencing their taste. Of course, in part this was made possible by a higher average standard of living, but the increase in inland trade led to the greater prominence of the middleman in the arts as well as in other forms of merchandise. Picture restorers and dealers, and auctioneers took their place beside the older established middlemen of the book trade. Like middlemen in other fields, the dealer in pictures and prints usually found it more profitable than being a creative artist. Once again the dominance of London was obvious, and became more so as better communications reduced the time-lag in the spread of fashions from the south-east to the north-west.

Emphasis has already been laid on the urban section of the population because the towns inevitably played a major part in stimulating a wider interest in the arts. In the first place, though population growth in the country as a whole had slowed down in the second half of the seventeenth century, many towns had continued to grow and this growth, combined with an increase in wealth, pushed up the demand for services and manufactured goods. These included the craft and luxury trades, and it is among them that the products of the decorative arts are found: gold, silverware, clocks, furniture, textiles, leatherwork, pottery, glass. There were not just more people in the towns, there were more who were able to indulge in conspicuous consumption: successful businessmen, professionals like physicians or attorneys, and minor gentry who preferred to be the leaders of an urban élite rather than low in the ranks of the county landowning society.

Secondly, the larger city could provide some support for the live arts of theatre and music. In fact, in the 1690s only London had any regular public theatre. Before 1682 there had been two rival companies, but they were forced by economic necessity into a merger for several years until a group split away in 1695 (see p. 57). It is indicative of the small circle of patrons (and perhaps also of the nature of the contemporary drama) that a city of half a million found two theatres almost too much to support. Outside London there were groups of players moving round from town to town on regular circuits. The established comedians were based on a regional centre such as Norwich or York, and timed their visits to coincide with occasions such as the assizes or a race meeting that brought society into the town. Spas like Tunbridge Wells and Bath also attracted the players, and Bath had its first purpose-built theatre in 1705. The provincial theatre was still insecure, its players poor, its performances in makeshift surroundings, its most successful companies dependent still on a nobleman's personal support, yet urban society in the new spas and the older regional capitals was increasingly able to enjoy the latest plays from London. In music the pattern was similar, though public concerts were unknown before the 1670s. By the end of the century, however, they were an established part of the London scene, with the familiar commercial features of agents, advertisements and publishing. The 1690s was a crucial decade in the substitution of public for private patronage.

In the third place, it was in the towns that the idea of patronage by subscription took root. As we have already seen, public subscriptions contributed to great undertakings like St Paul's and Greenwich, but the principle was widely adopted to finance other cultural projects. It was a new kind of group patronage, for it did not depend on membership of a particular corporation or guild. Anyone who had the means could subscribe to a new book, a monthly music publication, a particular play production. Nothing better illustrates the growth of urban middle classes who now had the money and leisure to pursue those cultural interests hitherto the preserve of nobility and gentry. Of course the gentry were subscribing patrons, too, and this was yet another way in which the attitudes of the gentry were aped by the aspiring groups below. It is significant that this method of public patronage should have expanded in the 1690s. Just as the war was financed on loans from a wide number of people looking for reliable investment, so on a smaller scale cultural activities were supported on credit. And lastly, the urban route whereby London influence was spread throughout the country was becoming as important as the country-house route. Great landowners were innovators in architecture, but provincial towns copied the fashionable London house of brick and eagerly followed the latest styles in dress or furniture. The growth of the provincial presses after the lapse of the Licensing Act in 1695 (see p. 75) did not lessen the capital's influence: they served rather as convenient outlets for London news. New spa towns admittedly provided a facility for London society that was not to be found in the capital, but they were otherwise just an extension of London society at play. Music and dancing, as well as gambling, went down unaltered to Tunbridge Wells and were quickly followed by shops 'full of all sorts of toys, silver, china, milliners, and all sorts of curious wooden ware' as Celia Fiennes recorded in her journal. The same process was at work in the other towns and cities. Provincial urban society wanted to be up to date, and there was no other lead to follow but London's.

However, it would be a mistake to underestimate the strength of vernacular custom in resisting the inroads of London influence. Only twenty per cent of the total population lived in towns of more than one thousand people, and half of these were concentrated in London, so that the great majority lived in rural surroundings. Again, as we have seen, only half the population had money to spare beyond subsistence. The impact of individual towns on their neighbourhoods is difficult to assess in more than general terms. Even today the physical appearance of some villages has withstood the powerful solvents of industrial society. It is possible, however, to suggest those areas of life where the vernacular still left its mark on the arts. Geographically, it was the remote upland areas of the country that were the strongholds of vernacular tradition. But villages only a few miles from a town or from a busy trade route could be just as isolated. Even in the south-east there were villages where crafts and customs succumbed only to the motor-car. So we are concerned here with very persistent traditions. Firstly it should be noted that the commonest area of vernacular strength in the arts was in building. By the end of the seventeenth century classical influence, having conquered the great house a century earlier, was victorious over the style of the medium-sized manor house or farmhouse (with a handful of exceptions in the remote north and west). Materials were another matter, and until the dramatic revolution in transport few builders could afford not to use local materials. So we find a house like Wallington in Northumberland built in local sandstone, or Ven House in Somerset built in brick from local clay on the site, yet both in classical style. Cottages, farm outbuildings, boundary walls, however, remained vernacular in style and materials. Secondly, some of the rural and urban crafts withstood the pressure for change and maintained their own character. Hoskins has referred to the group of plasterers in north Devon in the later seventeenth century as a regional school, and claims they were producing work as good as anything else in England. Similarly the masons of the Cotswold chest-tombs have given us distinctive regional types that persisted for more than a century[68].

Thirdly, local tradition remained strong in the arts of the home. Needle and the woodworker's chisel were often employed to produce gifts for weddings and christenings. Social custom has always been particularly strong in rituals associated with birth, marriage and death. Wedding gifts, especially, have given us examples of popular (and, of course, of sophisticated) art, and often these have survived because they were treasured both for sentimental reasons and for their intrinsic value. The variety is wide: decorative pottery plates, wooden boxes, embroidered coverlets, carved cupboards. They often incorporate the initials of the bridal pair and the year of marriage. Funeral customs have left us with hatchments; birth ceremonies with christening robes or presentation pieces of silver.

Seasonal celebrations have had less effect in tangible terms. Feasting is ephemeral, and decorative efforts on food, or house or church were perishable. There has also been a poor survival rate for the arts of dance and music which must have played a major part in such festivities. Here we are in an area where dating is difficult and exact information impossible. Nor are we much better off when it comes to the popular arts of the fairs of this time. There are descriptions of some of the great annual Fairs like Stourbridge and Bartholomew's, and we know the titles of some of the drolls and puppet shows produced. But folk drama, like ballads and broadsheets, has really only survived by accident for few people were interested in preserving something which had no literary merit. The ephemeral art of the procession was also vulnerable. Royal processions attracted artists and there are engravings, for example, of William and Mary's Coronation procession. We also have some record of the spectacular pageants of the Lord Mayor's Show. But of the popular forms of dance and song that accompanied such civic events we know nothing definite. Popular arts connected with religious festivals had, of course, been swept away by the Reformation, and civic ceremonies were a pale substitute. Some, like the Godiva procession at Coventry, were conscious revivals, not the outcome of indigenous tradition. On the other hand, the village maypole and the dancing round it seem to have reappeared quickly after the Puritan banning during the Commonwealth and, according to Defoe, had a further revival at the beginning of Anne's reign.

Traditional customs have always been weakened by the spread of education, and the extent of literacy has obviously affected the arts of a society. How literate was the England of William and Mary? After a probable sharp rise in literacy in the century before the Civil War (noticeable in the towns and especially in London where over half the male population may have been literate) there seems to have been a levelling, even a falling off, in the second half of the seventeenth century. Educational expansion ceased in most towns after the Restoration, no doubt partly explained by the slowing down in the population growth, and only began again when the first charity schools were founded at the end of the century. There are, of course, no statistics on literacy, and evidence in this field is fragmentary. What can be said about the later seventeenth century is that there was a large market for the broadsheet ballad[10, 34]

HEt colours bjabely to dilplay,
    fhe often had the luck,
And was at pufh of Pike fome fay,
    as good as eber ftruck:
To fold her Arms, and furl the Flag

Thus cunningly the time fhe paff,
    and none did her detect,
Until the Souldiers at the laft
    began foj to fulpect:
And by fome certain figns in fhojt,

10. Woodcut on a broadsheet ballad *The Female Warrior*

and this indicates that among the buyers there were people who could read even though there were wooodcuts to appeal to those who could not and a familiar tune to which the new words could be sung. Similarly the cheap little chapbook satisfied a need for potted tales again enlivened with naive woodcuts. It was a market that had nothing in common with the literature or engravings aimed at the educated classes, and yet there were occasional cross-links. A good tune was common to theatre and market square, and some of the broadsheet ballads were set to 'a play-house tune'. It was some years, however, before Gay deliberately scored his opera with ballad tunes and brought the native tradition back to the stage as a challenge to the take-over by Italian opera. Popular art which is non-literate can only flourish naturally where speech and pictures have not been degraded as forms of communication and where there are enough people who can only communicate in this way. An upper-class literate culture does not necessarily destroy the other though it can drive it underground and discredit it in the eyes of would-be climbers.

If the lack of education in one part of society can influence the vigour of popular art so, too, the kind of education available to another part can affect the form of sophisticated art. Not only can ideas of art be disseminated, particularly by the printed word and by engravings, but the

11. A political cartoon of 1688

kind of education that is given to leaders of society will have important effects on patronage and the kind of art promoted. And, of course, the education and training that artists receive will be of great significance to the art they produce. Before we look a little more closely at the latter, let me underline the important role that education played in the formation of taste of the patron. The classical education that all sons of the aristocracy and gentry received, and the Grand Tour with its emphasis on Italy that the wealthy now increasingly enjoyed, tended to form artistic taste in a strongly similar mould. Of course, there were those whose links and interests lay elsewhere, and we shall see some of the results of Dutch influence in the next chapter, but this common classical base contributed to the completeness of the Palladian victory in the eighteenth century. Moreover, the Grand Tour itself brought many works of art back to England and stimulated collectors. The patronage of art was fashionable because the social élite regarded culture as a badge of its membership.

What of the training of the artists themselves? At the end of the seventeenth century there were no academies of art as in France, no professional education for painters or architects or sculptors. Though the idea of an academy of painting had been mooted earlier it was not till 1711 that one was established in London under Kneller's direction. The alternatives were an apprenticeship with a master craftsman or in the studio of some well known artist or seeking instruction abroad. For the question first raised in fifteenth-century Italy remained: what was the artist's position in society? Was he just a skilled artisan or had he some professional status which entitled him to greater respect and reward? In seventeenth-century England successful artists could climb the social ladder in much the same way as successful tradesmen or civil servants. Leading painters were knighted: Rubens and Van Dyck by Charles I, Lely by Charles II and Kneller by William III. So were architects in the second half of the century: Pratt and Wren, and Vanbrugh a little later (it is interesting that whereas these were English the painters were all foreigners). Evelyn numbered artists among his friends; Vanbrugh was welcome in the homes of many of the aristocracy. But social success for a few individuals does not cover up the fact that many more remained working craftsmen all their lives. The outmoded guild system was not completely dead, for apprenticeships were still the entry to the building trades and to such crafts as carving and gilding and decorative painting. These drew their recruits from the manual working class though the Painter-Stainers Company occasionally included a 'gentleman'. In particular, the great mason–sculptors of the late seventeenth century all came from such a background: Edward Pierce was the son of a decorative painter, John Bushnell of a plumber and William Stanton carried on his uncle's mason's yard. No English gentleman it seems regarded sculpture as a suitable occupation for his sons, nor does it appear to have attracted gentlemen-amateurs, as they were drawn to painting or architecture. Painting had long been a suitable leisure pursuit for women as well as men, and the later seventeenth century produced two amateur painters of some repute in Mary Beale and Joan Carlile. Architecture as an amateur's field, however, reached the highest level at the turn of the century with an amateur of genius in Vanbrugh. While it was not unusual for landowners to design their own houses (a practice that continued into the eighteenth century) Vanbrugh was commissioned by the Earl of Carlisle to design Castle Howard when he had had no architectural experience at all. Luckily his inventive genius was matched by Hawksmoor's technical skill, and this partnership proved immensely fruitful. Hawksmoor had been trained under Wren in the Office of Works, and this was a kind of apprenticeship that amounted virtually to professional training. Lowly-paid clerks (Hawksmoor was still earning only two shillings a day after seven years in the Office) were grounded in the basic skills of drawing and design and could rise to responsible posts within the Works and thence to commissions outside. Wren could well claim at the end of his long tenure of the post of Surveyor-General that 'whatever the clerks may have been formerly, they are now required to be well skilled in all kinds of admeasurement, in drawing, making plans of all the palaces, and taking elevations, and completely versed in all parts of architecture ... likewise knowing in the goodness, choice and value of all sorts of materials'. This was apprenticeship of a different order from that to be found in the building trades. It was the elements of design and invention that offered a training far above the technical skills that could be learned from a mason or carpenter. Much of the building all over the country was in the hands of such contracting-craftsmen who could copy but not innovate. So the role of the Office of Works was crucial. Wren gathered round him a team of craftsmen who worked on the royal palaces, at Chelsea and Greenwich, and on St Paul's and the City churches, but underneath was the efficient organisation of the Office which made possible these tremendous undertakings. As a missionary force for spreading architectural styles and high standards of craftsmanship it was unrivalled. It also established the architect as a man with professional status.

The Chapel Royal offered a somewhat similar apprenticeship in music. Choristers came from cathedrals all over the country to fill the twelve coveted places, and beyond their general education and vocal training were taught musical composition and a variety of instruments. Even when the boys' voices broke their education was continued and many became Gentlemen of the Chapel Royal. There was no better introduction to a musical career. Humfrey and Blow and both Purcell brothers were all children of the Chapel Royal. Like the Office of Works, the training was far more than an instruction in technique. It offered the stimulus of a creative environment where a new school of composers was making the Chapel Royal the centre of musical interest in the country (see p. 87). With the death of Charles II, however, it lost this pre-eminence, though it continued to train musicians. Outside the Chapel Royal and the cathedral schools there were plenty of private professional teachers, for music was a valued accomplishment. But there was a growing gulf between the domestic music enjoyed as a social activity and concert music played by the professional for public entertainment. As the continental fashion for virtuosi players and singers gained ground so the line between amateur and professional hardened.

Academies for the arts of painting and music were to be established long before any schools of dramatic art. The writing of plays was no disparagement to a gentleman (and in England after the Restoration most were written by those within the Court circle), but the acting of them on the public stage undoubtedly was. So a player joined a company and learnt his trade as best he might. Colley Cibber was nine months in the 'lowest Rank' of the Theatre Royal Company before he was accepted on the payroll – at ten shillings a week. He was lucky in being supported by his father, the notable sculptor (see p. 151), who, despite his disapproval of his son's choice of career when there was the possibility of some government 'place' through the Duke of Devonshire's influence, continued to give him a yearly allowance of twenty pounds. Colley Cibber was not the only actor of such respectable background, but he himself noted in his autobiography that the profession was widely despised. At the top, however, success and 'irreproachable' behaviour could win an actor or actress social acceptance.

Social acceptance was the aim of every climber in English society, and at a time when the opportunities for social advancement were greater than they had been in the middle years of the century it was fortunate for the artist and craftsman that social acceptance included the patronage of the arts. But it was fortunate, too, for them that there was a spread of interest in the arts and a broader-based patronage in urban society as well as from the landed gentry. This wider interest did not equal the extraordinary appetite for works of art among the ordinary people that Evelyn had noticed in Holland in the 1640s. But many foreign artists saw their opportunity in the growing prosperity of England and were not disappointed. The 1690s proved to be a time of expansion and great variety in the arts. Architecture boasted not only the new style Chatsworth and Castle Howard[52, 5] but the old style manor house of Tadworth Court[58] and the Gothic revival of the parish church at Warwick. Music lovers could go to both English-style operas with masques and the new Italian singers at York Buildings. Theatre supporters could see the new 'sentimental' plays as well as the highlights of Restoration drama. In furniture, silver and glass, new styles were appearing to add to the diversity. And yet this appearance of variety hides an undercurrent of uniformity that came to the surface in the eighteenth century. It was a uniformity of taste that took its cue from the dominance of the gentry in English society. Their influence was pervasive not only in the counties but also in the provincial towns and in the capital. The cultural life of the cities like York and Norwich, the social life of the new spas, the academic life of Oxford and Cambridge were all, as much as the activities of the country house, part of the same fashionable pattern: the response to the interests of the landed classes who moved easily from a London season to the country and back again. Of course there were exceptions, but in general the twin dominance of London and the gentry is the key to this uniformity of taste in the eighteenth century.

The Revolution of 1688

During the dozen years that followed the Revolution there were significant changes in many areas of English life: in politics with the shift of power from Crown to Parliament, in government with the emergence of a workable Cabinet system and the expansion of the professional civil service, in the realm of high finance and public credit, in new relationships with the Continent, in religious matters and in the new freedom for press and publisher. Some of these cannot be separated from the demands of continuous war with France, but neither can the struggle with Louis XIV be isolated from the invitation to William III. To William the English Crown meant greater resources in his life-long battle to contain French power. So the Revolution and its more revolutionary aftermath is not just a convenient dividing point. The innovations were decisive. Later admirers of the Glorious Revolution saw it as the restoration of law, liberties and property, and of the Church, all of which had been threatened by James II. In fact, the legitimate king and his heir were set aside and another substituted with limited power and financially dependent on an annual parliament.

William landed in Torbay in November 1688, invited by a group of influential men to head their rebellion against the Catholic policies of the King. As William's army moved slowly towards London James's supporters melted away and in late December the King fled to France. The Convention Parliament was elected in February and deliberated for three weeks. It declared the throne to be vacant, and since William made it clear that he would not stay as Mary's consort the Crown was offered jointly to them both. Mary came over from Holland to join her husband, and on 23 February they formally accepted the offer of the throne on the terms laid down in the Declaration of Rights. These curtailed the

Crown's prerogative so disastrously exercised by James. Parliamentary and not divine right now gave title to the Crown, and William swore to govern 'according to the statutes in Parliament agreed on'. From now on the Crown as well as the people were under the rule of law. The courts ceased to be used by the monarch for political purposes, and the judges' tenure was secured against royal interference, first by William's voluntary action and then by the Act of Settlement. William, however, had no wish to have the royal prerogative pruned beyond James's excesses. It took several years before he would agree to triennial parliamentary elections, for example, and then only under pressure of the crisis of war. The war and its unprecedented demands on the public purse determined the course of the constitutional settlement. William could not conduct the war without money from Parliament, and Parliament used this power to impose further limits on the Crown. On the other hand the war could not be fought without strengthening the position of the executive. The administration expanded rapidly and with it grew the importance of the professional civil servant. As a link between the executive and the legislature the Cabinet developed to coordinate the tasks of wartime planning, and to give Queen Mary systematic advice when William was out of the country. It was fully accepted by the time Anne came to the throne, but William remained its master and appointed its members. He was autocratic by nature and only necessity made him a constitutional monarch. Foreign affairs and military matters he kept to himself. No one disputed the Crown's right to decide foreign policy, and William assumed control here with almost no lessening of authority. Even those Whigs who wanted to curb the royal powers further found themselves behind the King in the war against France and quite unable to approach his knowledge of European affairs. Yet nothing was possible without parliamentary money. Clashes were inevitable, but after many years of political instability a balance between Crown and Parliament was achieved. The Crown learnt how to influence politics through patronage, and Parliament how to play its financial card effectively. A workable system of constitutional monarchy was hammered out during the most expensive war England had ever fought.

The Revolution brought a dramatic reversal in English foreign policy. Charles II had allied with France, and James II, even if he was no puppet of Louis XIV, had shown no concern for French advance in Europe. The immediate effect of William's accession was the declaration of war against France in May 1689. England was drawn into European politics, and for more than a hundred years enmity against France and the balance of power on the Continent became the guiding principles of English foreign policy. This meant a permanent involvement in European affairs. William's new subjects did not need persuading that Louis XIV's policies were a threat to their national security. They were less concerned at first with European equilibrium than with the danger to the Protestant Succession and the threat of James II's return 'with Popery at his heels and the French king riding on his back'. Hence the demand at the Peace of Ryswick for Louis XIV's acknowledgement of William's title and the renewal of war in 1701 on Louis's recognition of the Old Pretender as James III. The decisive move, however, had been taken: England was now committed to intervention on the Continent.

If the Revolution of 1688 was such a decisive political event what was its place in the history of English arts? Was the shift of power from Crown to Parliament reflected in the patterns of patronage? Did the dramatic change in foreign policy have its counterpart in artistic fashion? With William of Orange on the throne was Dutch influence substituted for that of France? And how were the arts affected by the Toleration Act which put an end to religious persecution? There are no simple answers to these questions. The interaction of political, religious and artistic changes is always complex and this was the case with the English reaction to European styles at the end of the seventeenth century.

The central problem is the extent of baroque influence in England. The full baroque style of the Continent was never completely adopted here but something of its spirit infected nearly every area of the arts at the end of the century. The essence of baroque lies in its stress on the dramatic to portray and arouse emotion. It always has a sense of movement and a delight in illusion. It makes a total impact whether in a building and its setting or the treatment of an interior. With a few notable exceptions (some of which will be referred to in the following chapters) the baroque influence was modified in England and absorbed into the more restrained native tradition. Of course it was not totally dominant on the Continent. The classical tradition was never submerged and acted as a brake on the exuberance of the full-blown baroque. In Holland, for instance, the style of sculpture and architecture was a fusion of these two strands; and the same tension between the opposing tendencies with a similar resolution can be found in England. Here, however, the baroque influence was late arriving. It can be seen in stone monuments soon after the Restoration, and in the works of foreign decorative painters for Charles II and James II but architecture was unaffected till the 1690s, and music only slightly earlier. By the time England had overcome her

12. A minor example of baroque wood-carving

isolation from the main stream of European artistic development, a stage which coincided with her new role of political intervention in Europe, the age of eighteenth-century classicism was about to begin.

Throughout the seventeenth century the King and the Court were the major agents for introducing European styles into this country. As we have seen in the previous chapter the Crown was the greatest single source

13. Delftware charger with portrait of Queen Mary: Brislington (diameter 34 cm)

of patronage and this was unaffected by the constitutional changes of
1689. Whoever succeeded James II would have had unrivalled personal
influence in setting fashions and attitudes and the opportunity to
patronise the arts through posts in the Household, personal commissions
and government projects. William's own interests in the arts were limited.
He did not share the enthusiasm of Charles II for the theatre or music

and his personal qualities were not such as to make him a leader of fashion. He was too withdrawn and serious minded, and in any case his passions and energy were concentrated on the war with Louis XIV. He spent very little time in England. Every summer till the peace of 1697 he was with the army on campaign and thereafter he spent several months each year in Holland. He shared an interest however with the Queen in the furnishing of the royal palaces and in their gardens. Together they had enjoyed the planning and refurbishing of their Dutch residences and together they turned their attention to the alterations of the English royal palaces. Mary's own interests were probably wider. Wren was impressed with her taste and knowledge, and her death brought the work at Hampton Court to a standstill. She patronised the theatre a little and there is some evidence that she was anxious to improve the standard of church music by creating a new post of composer for the Chapel Royal. Her devotion to the skills of embroidery and to the collection of porcelain and delftware was well known. It is impossible, however, to describe the accession of William and Mary as a take-over by Dutch fashions. The introduction of Dutch taste in furniture, pottery and garden design was balanced by French-inspired decorative painting, ironwork and silver. While in Holland William and Mary were in close touch with French styles and this link had been strengthened by the many Huguenot refugees in the Netherlands. Some of these Huguenot craftsmen and designers followed William to England, swelling the number already here.

This pinpoints the difficulty of linking artistic change with politics. There was no neat correlation between alliances with France or Holland and their influence on English arts. All through the reign of Charles II, when a pro-French policy was pursued and French fashions were followed at court, Dutch influence remained consistently strong. Commercial rivalry and war did not prevent the adoption of Dutch artistic ideas. Nor did war against Louis XIV result in the rejection of French styles. The Sun King was identified with popery and arbitrary power but he was also the centre of the most magnificent court in Europe which was still the undisputed leader of fashion and culture. Patriotism in the seventeenth century did not extend to the condemnation of the arts of a military opponent. On the other hand personal contacts with Holland were obviously strengthened by the Revolution. The maintenance of an army in the Low Countries brought many Englishmen to Holland and some of them like William Blathwayt, the King's Secretary at War, bought paintings, books and furniture for their English homes (see p. 133). In the other direction came William's Dutch favourites, such as

Bentinck and Keppel. To a certain extent the war dislocated contacts with France but they were quickly renewed with the peace in 1697 and pictures and prints were bought in Paris for English collectors. Moreover knowledge of French styles continued to be spread through pattern books and engravings. On the other hand, the prohibitions on French imports during the war and the later heavy duties had a more permanent effect in the area of decorative arts. Protection gave native manufacture of luxuries such as silk a chance to expand, though the influx of Huguenots ensured a close copy of French styles. The Protestant refugees had begun to settle in England well before the Revocation of the Edict of Nantes in 1685 but the Revolution and the war against France made them welcome and encouraged their integration in English society. There was enthusiasm for raising funds for their support and large numbers obtained letters of naturalisation even though there was a certain amount of resentment against the newcomers among English craftsmen. The Huguenots made a notable contribution to such industries as the making of silk, linen, paper and glass, and in the skilled crafts of silversmithing and ironwork. Indeed

14. Huguenot style silver wine-cistern (height 22 cm, width 56 cm)

there were few industries that were not affected by the influx of French ideas and expertise. As many as seventy thousand Huguenots were said to have settled in England, Ireland and the colonies and of these a considerable proportion came to London. Daniel Marot the designer, Jean Tijou the ironsmith, David Willaume the silversmith, and the gunsmith Pierre Monlong are four of the better known[78, 80, 81, 82]. These acted as more than a leaven of skill: they were influential in establishing new styles in their respective fields, styles which all originated in France. It should be emphasised that Huguenots were not the only foreigners working in England. Foreign artists were found in every branch of the arts except perhaps literature and in most were the pace-setters. The leading portrait painter came from Lübeck; the sculptor Cibber from Denmark and Grinling Gibbons from the Low Countries; Italian singers and French dancers were applauded on the stage; and in all the decorative arts, except glass and embroidery as far as we know, there were craftsmen from the Continent. England for them was the land of opportunity. They formed the chief way in which change in artistic style came to England. On the whole it can be said that the balance between Dutch and French influence in the arts was even. The Revolution certainly extended the period of Dutch influence in England and it is possible that the war with France increased interest in Italy and may have hastened the classical movement of the eighteenth century. Above all, the Revolution made England a European power and so helped to establish her cultural leadership after the defeat of the French in the long war.

The most obvious impact of the Revolution in the area of the arts was the destruction of the royal Catholic chapels. James's chapel in Whitehall in particular was a magnificent example of full-blown baroque where all the senses were aroused in the service of the liturgy and its setting. Here was religious art of the kind familiar to Catholic France or Italy. Did its close association with the arbitrary policies of the Stuart Kings, as well as with Catholicism, halt the spread of the baroque style? Just possibly it did. Opposition to display and decoration in Anglican churches may well have been stiffened. Only in the private chapels of colleges or noblemen where the restraints of parish churches did not apply was the baroque spirit found. There are very fine baroque interiors at Chatsworth[15] and Trinity College, Oxford (see p. 162). The most remarkable example was the chapel at Petworth, where the family pew was designed in the form of a theatre box, with the painted illusion of a curtain drawn aside to allow the spectators to see the show. It would be difficult to find a more explicit statement of the link between baroque art and the theatre. The royal chapels, by contrast, became models of decorum in their decoration; and the music was shorn of its violin players and reduced to what was considered a suitable style for worship (see p. 91). Outside the chapel, however, there was no rejection of the baroque style by William III.

William was just as conscious as his predecessors that art can be used to glorify the monarchy. Once the Catholic flavour had been eliminated (and one of the results of the Revolution was the removal of Catholics

15. A baroque interior: the Chapel, Chatsworth House

such as Verrio or Dryden from official posts) then art could be enlisted
as propaganda for the Revolution, and baroque art with its emphasis on
display was the perfect medium. The symbolism could not embrace the
Martyr-King nor the Divine Right of Kings but William as Hercules
could declare the triumph of Protestantism. This is the theme of much
of the decoration of Hampton Court (see p. 124) and shows that the style
was hardly touched by the Revolution. William and Mary continued, too,
the tradition of royal processions and pageantry and their subjects still
gave royal portraits as a token of loyalty. It seemed that a constitutional
monarch could make almost as much use of art as an absolute king.

A constitutional monarch, however, shares power with a parliament
and this shift was indeed reflected in the pattern of patronage. William

might commission great artists at Hampton Court but the Duke of Devonshire could command the same for his new palace at Chatsworth. So too could the Duke of Somerset at Petworth, and Exeter at Burghley and Carlisle at Castle Howard. The Revolution was a triumph for the small group of aristocratic families whose wealth came mainly from land and whose political authority was established by the control of government patronage. Places in the gift of the Crown and government (and the war created more of these) were increasingly bestowed by ministers, and though much of this patronage was political in purpose the arts were drawn into the same pattern. The Crown began to lose its predominance in artistic patronage and the initiative passed into the hands of the aristocracy. It is highly significant that the Palladian revolution when it came was hatched and carried through by Burlington and his friends. Innovations like this in the seventeenth century came from within the royal circle. William's own lack of interest in the arts was partly responsible; more important, because it was not dependent on the personality of the monarch, was the shift of power from Crown to the landed magnates.

In political terms land meant power in Parliament, and this involved the gentry in the Commons as well as the aristocracy in the Lords. The period after 1688 was one of intense political activity. Divisions between Whig and Tory, Court and Country, produced a turmoil of party faction. Annual parliaments and frequent elections kept the controversies at fever pitch. How did this parliamentary and party activity affect the arts? In the first place the increase in elections, including the hearing of disputed ones by the House of Commons, brought more people to London. This emphasised the role of London as a capital and increased its leadership in culture and the arts. In the second place, the political factions kept the London presses busy with pamphlets and cartoons and gave employment to some of England's great literary figures. This was the forcing ground of Swift, Steele and Defoe and out of it came the new literary journalism and the successes of *The Tatler* and *The Spectator*. Thirdly, the political parties created their own artistic circles with the Kit-Kat Club (see p. 101) and the Tory group round the Earl of Oxford. Artists mixed on equal terms with the politicians and out of such clubs came Kneller's famous series of portraits[16] and many of Vanbrugh's commissions. This was the kind of artistic circle which usurped the role of the Stuart Court. Before the eighteenth century there does not seem to have been any distinction between the art of the two groups: there is no connotation between Toryism and a Dahl portrait or between Whiggism and a Vanbrugh play. This is not surprising while the lines between the parties

16. Vanbrugh by Kneller: painted for the Kit-Kat Club

were so confused. Early ministries of William's reign were 'mixed' and the divisions between Court and Country cut across those of Whig and Tory. Though the Whigs later claimed the Revolution as their own it could not have been achieved without the Tories. It was their revolt against James's policies that turned the day. While politics was in such a state of flux there could be no 'Tory' or 'Whig' art. Only with the Whig adoption of Palladianism in the eighteenth century and the Tories' continued allegiance to baroque was such a division possible. The Whig aristocrats in the 1690s commissioned baroque artists as readily as anyone else. No more than the Crown did they reject the style which had been so closely associated with the hated Stuart policies. Had the Revolution been a social upheaval as well as a constitutional one, then the continuity in artistic development might have been threatened. As it was, the changes were more evident in patterns of patronage than in styles.

What were the effects on the arts of the financial changes of the 1690s? Did the demands of the war economy, for instance, reduce spending in this area? The cost of the war with France was far greater than any previous one and in an effort to find the money to pay the bills new taxes and a completely new system of public credit were developed. This financial revolution made lending to the government safe and profitable, and bridged the gap between income and expenditure of over £1 million a year. The foundation of the Bank of England and the exploitation of the nation's credit created a new 'moneyed interest' in the City increasingly at conflict with the landed interest of the country as a whole. The land tax was a heavy burden not shared by owners of other kinds of property and it hit the landowners during a period of poor harvests and falling rents. It probably had less effect on consumption in the area of the arts than might have been expected. Status was judged by appearances and there were plenty of families prepared to mortgage their properties before they would consider altering their style of living. The new moneyed interest was predominantly London-based and found investment in the funds more profitable than land. As many were self-made men they made a significant addition to the pool of possible urban patrons. Fortunes were also made by office-holders and in contracts for the Army and Navy, and these new rich were the status-seeking spenders discussed in chapter 1. Sometimes it was a local community that benefited from the profits of war as Rochester did with the gift of a new town hall from the Admiral, Sir Clowdisley Shovell. Moreover the close connection between wealth and patronage of the arts meant that any expansion of the economy was likely to increase the opportunities for patronage. The war caused shifts in the pattern of trade, with certain European ports closed to English shipping, but the dislocation was more than offset by the general stimulus to the economy. The expansion of the Army and Navy, for example, brought work to the shipyards, the foundries and the heavy woollen industry. The manufacture of luxuries was, as we have seen, encouraged by high import duties. There was an incentive to discover new techniques as the patent boom of the 1690s indicates. Above all, the economy was boosted by the new exploitation of credit.

Beyond its political and economic effects the Revolution had a religious dimension and the impact of the Toleration Act on the arts must now be examined. The hostile reaction of the mob to the Catholic chapels has already been noted and of course the Protestant Succession was the cornerstone of the constitutional settlement. James II had tried to win the support of the dissenters by his policy of general toleration. He failed because the great majority were as strongly opposed as the Anglicans to James's Catholicism. The 1689 Act which rewarded the Protestant dissenters for their backing of the Revolution was only a grudging recognition of their existence and suspended rather than repealed the penal provisions of the Clarendon Code. Dissenters were allowed to worship in their own meeting-houses provided the doors were unlocked and the places registered with the bishop or Quarter Sessions. They were still debarred from holding municipal or public offices. However, the Act was widely interpreted and has always been called a Toleration Act. The dissenters now had a legal status in the community: the idea of 'comprehension' in the National Church was abandoned and new meeting-houses began to go up all over the country. In the first year licences were issued

17. Friars Street Meeting-House, Ipswich, 1699

for seven hundred and ninety-six temporary and one hundred and forty-three permanent meeting-houses, and two hundred and thirty-nine further places for the Quakers. The number of congregations grew and their total membership was about a tenth of the population. They were stronger in London and the provincial cities and may have been as much as a third of the populations of Norwich, Bristol, Birmingham and Exeter. Though there were still dissenters among the gentry and some powerful voices in Parliament, the social disabilities proved too great for them and by 1714 the sects were predominantly urban, and middle and lower class. What effect on the arts had this sizeable community and their newly-won liberties? In the first place, most obviously, there are the kind of buildings they erected. Many of the meeting-houses were converted private dwellings and furnished simply with pulpit, table and surrounding benches. Others were purpose-built but with no more elaboration than a substantial cottage. Only their single storey and the line of windows disclosed their function. A few of the city meeting-houses, however, were large and, within the confines of Puritan worship, beautifully equipped, like the one at Friars Street, Ipswich[17] or the Old Meeting-house in Norwich. These were exceptional: plain exteriors and furniture, and plain headstones in the burial ground, were the usual pattern. The same approach governed the attitude to music. It was a distraction from worship and the stricter congregations even condemned the singing of metrical psalms. However, it was from this background that Isaac Watts, the first great English hymn writer, arose and the revival in congregational singing began (see p. 93). It is impossible to define a dissenting approach to design but the affinities of the dissenters with the Dutch Protestants may have strengthened the links with Holland and so the acceptance of Dutch styles. They may also have stiffened the English reaction to Catholic-flavoured baroque and hastened the movement against the highly decorated styles in furniture and other arts. In the second place, the dissenters condemned the theatre and with their large numbers in London must have been one of the factors that kept the audience small. Opposition to the playhouses on moral grounds was not of course restricted to the dissenters; and the famous blast against the stage came from the pen of one of the Anglican Nonjurors (see p. 71). It was, however, the Puritan strand in English life that they so clearly represented. In the third place, the acceptance of toleration in religious matters opened the way to rationalism and a more open intellectual climate. Apart from the great controversy between natural and revealed religion that ensued, the rational spirit can be seen in the new kinds of literature that flourished in the less dogmatic atmosphere: the secular essay, literary journals, the sentimental drama. The restraints were loosened – the Licensing Act lapsed in 1695 – and the 1690s saw new patterns of literary patronage established. For the first time in English history one can speak of a reading public, and writers who wished to keep in business were obliged to pay attention to the wants of their new patrons. There was a sudden expansion of publications of many kinds, answering the wide demands of a society with more wealth and more leisure: newspapers, magazines, children's books, primers of all sorts, luxury editions and cheap issues.

The Revolution was a landmark for the Church of England as well as for the dissenters and two further effects in the area of the arts should be noted here. The Church's authority was weakened on the one hand by the loss of the Nonjurors who refused to take the new oath of allegiance and on the other by the Toleration Act. The loss of confidence and a feeling of defensiveness were reflected in the small amount of building activity in the 1690s (with the exception of St Paul's) and perhaps the variety of styles adopted where rebuilding was being pursued illustrates the ambivalence in which many Anglicans found themselves. Secondly, the decline of the Chapel Royal as a centre of musical innovation was accelerated by the Revolution. Purcell and other composers turned to the theatre for inspiration and a gulf developed between church and secular music. It became accepted that only certain kinds of music were appropriate to worship: violins and gay tunes belonged to the theatre and not to a church.

This concern in the Church of England with decorum in the musical setting of worship was part of the same Protestant tradition that found its extreme form in a Quaker meeting-house. It is a reminder that the influences on the arts of the 1690s reach well back beyond the events of the Revolution and that the effects mentioned here are only part of the picture. The Revolution, for instance, played no part in ending the long period in architecture of transition from the Tudor vernacular style to the fully classical nor did it affect the influence of the East in the development of the chinoiserie style in the decorative arts. The strength of vernacular traditions would have delayed the acceptance of continental styles with or without the Revolution; and it was the expansion of overseas trade to Asia that produced the delightful hybrid decoration we call chinoiserie.

The following chapters will consider the arts separately but it should be noted that this makes arbitrary divisions, as, for example, in the decoration of an interior. Architecture, painting and sculpture in a baroque build-

18. Detail from a silk coverlet embroidered by Sarah Thurstone
with chinoiserie designs in brightly coloured silks and silver thread

ing need to be seen as one creation and some overlapping is inevitable. Moreover the discussion of individual arts tends to conceal similarities of design. The cartouche form, for example, found in wall monuments appears in bookplates and engraved titles[46]; chinoiserie figures are used on embroidery, silver and furniture[6, 18]; the French lambrequin or tas-selled-cloth motive appears in decorative ironwork and embroidery[81, 93]. Cross-references will be made where they seem helpful.

Drama and Literature

Any survey of the part played by drama in the society of late seventeenth-century England must include not only established playhouses in London but also the strolling players of the provinces and the popular stage at fairs: otherwise the picture is distorted. The booths of Bartholomew Fair did not present shows of literary merit and such drolls, as they were called, cannot be compared with a Congreve play. They are however evidence of the widespread delight in dramatic skill and remind us of the special role of the audience in this particular branch of the arts. Music needs to be performed, too, but the playing of a Purcell sonata, say, is complete in itself. The *raison d'être* of any dramatic performance is the audience. The audience in Drury Lane was very different from the group of spectators in front of a puppet booth yet each in its own way determined the kind of drama shown. Little is known of the activities of the provincial players in this period but it is clear that their repertoire depended on the London stage. Audiences in York or Norwich or Bath wanted to see plays that had had a success in the capital. For this reason the responses of the London audience assumed a wider significance.

The special interest of the 1690s lies in the effect on the stage of changes in society. On the surface there are many similarities between the Restoration playhouse of Charles II and that of William and Mary. The innovations that were brought in after the closure of the theatres during the Commonwealth were still the dominant influences in the theatre at the end of the century: the altered design of the playhouse, the use of changeable scenery and machines, the introduction of women as actresses, the insertion of songs and dances as entr'acte items of entertainment. The masterpieces of Congreve and Vanbrugh were a second flowering of the comedy of manners that found its first exponent in Etherege in the 1660s, and would have delighted the gallants of that earlier generation. Written to amuse, they seemed to accentuate the artificial nature of the theatre and its isolation from the real world outside. The spectators who laughed at the witty dialogue and comic situations seemed to be drawn from the same aristocratic circle as their predecessors had been and to their puritan critics seemed to take the same delight in bawdiness. The theatre however was not impervious to the changes around it. Though the comedies of Farquhar continue the Restoration tradition into the eighteenth century the movement for the reformation of manners was already taking effect in the 1690s. The comedy of wit, refined and polished and totally un-emotional, could not survive the inroads of sentiment. Congreve wrote no major play after 1700 when his best work *The Way of the World* had only a lukewarm reception. He felt that his kind of gentle satire on polite society and its mode of brilliant witty conversation was out of tune with the audience which was looking for sentimental comedy or crude farce. Both the audience and the playwrights who wrote for it were no longer as closely linked to the Court as they had been in the time of Charles II. There were more professional writers and a wider range among the spectators. They were open to the influence of changing social attitudes which the new journalism fostered and which rejected the pleasure-loving libertine values of the Restoration Court. The plays of Congreve, Van-brugh and Farquhar were the glorious final fling of Restoration comedy which could not survive in the respectable low-key world of *The Tatler*. The plays themselves however have never been forgotten and, after a prudish Victorian interlude, have often been performed on the modern stage. The farces and sentimental dramas which displaced them are by contrast quite rightly neglected.

There were two public theatres in use in London when William and Mary came to the throne, both built or rebuilt in the early 1670s. They were similar in size, the exterior measurements being one hundred and forty feet long and fifty-seven or fifty-eight feet wide (forty-three metres by eighteen metres). The one in Dorset Garden was more lavishly fitted than the Theatre Royal in Drury Lane and its auditorium even drew the praises of a French visitor for its beauty and convenience. Contemporary engravings which appeared in the 1673 edition of Settle's *The Empress of Morocco* show the entrance front and several different scenes behind its impressive proscenium[20]. In both theatres, in contrast to their Jaco-bean predecessors, the pit had become a main seating area (the benches in the Theatre Royal were even covered with cloth). At Dorset Garden there were two tiers of large boxes holding twenty persons each and a

19. William Congreve

gallery above. At the Theatre Royal the middle gallery does not seem to have been divided but in the alterations of 1696 some further boxes were constructed on the edge of the stage. The design encouraged an intimate and informal atmosphere in which chattering and flirting and even fighting could become more important than the play itself. The capacity of each playhouse is not known but may have been more than a thousand persons. A full house certainly meant severe overcrowding on the benches.

The design of the Restoration stage with its proscenium arch and sets of changeable scenery was very different from its Jacobean predecessor. The fore-stage, like the earlier apron stage, was the main acting area but,

20. Dorset Garden Theatre, proscenium arch and stage scenery for *The Empress of Morocco*

with the exception of those in the 1696 stage-boxes in the Theatre Royal, all the audience was in front of the stage and not round it. The scenic area behind the proscenium arch became increasingly important as the emphasis on spectacle grew. Scenes were changed by drawing the two portions of a flat apart on grooves revealing new splendours behind. Machines which, like movable scenery, originated in France, enabled goddesses to sail across the sky on clouds, or islands to rise out of the sea. By the 1690s the machinist could conjure up the most elaborate transformations. The stage directions for the first act of Settle's opera *The World in the Moon* in 1697 indicate the extravagant part that scenery and its mechanical shifters played in the theatre.

> 'Flat-Scene draws and discovers Three grand Arches of Clouds extending to the Roof of the House, terminated with a Prospect of Cloud-work, all fill'd with the Figures of Fames and Cupids; a Circular part of the back Clouds rolls softly away, and gradually discovers a Silver Moon, near Fourteen Foot Diameter: After which, the Silver Moon wanes off by degrees, and discovers the World within, consisting of Four grand Circles of Clouds, illustrated with Cupids, etc. Twelve Golden Chariots are seen riding in the Clouds, fill'd with Twelve Children, representing the Twelve Celestial Signs. The Third Arch intirely rolling away, leaves the full Prospect terminating with a large Lanschape of Woods, Waters, Towns, etc.'

Even though scenery was re-used the staging of such spectacular shows was very expensive. For example, the outlay on scenes, clothes and music for Purcell's *Fairy Queen* in 1692 was said to be £3000. The need to attract audiences had led to this increased expenditure on display and in-solvency had been one of the reasons for the uniting of the two companies in 1682.

Originally known as the King's Company and the Duke's Company they had royal patents giving them together a monopoly of acting in London. When they united they continued to use both theatres, staging the dramatic operas at Dorset Garden and the less ambitious productions at Drury Lane. Union was only a temporary answer to dwindling audiences and brought other problems as well. There were personal disputes between the actors and the management that could not be resolved and in the end led to a break-away by a substantial number of the company. The basis of the disagreement was financial. The new patentees had less personal interest in the theatre and regarded it as a speculation. When receipts at the door failed to bring in enough money they suggested

21. Thomas Betterton, mezzotint engraving

cutting salaries and even defrauded the actors. They tried to attract audiences by staging expensive operas such as Dryden's *The Prophetess* and *King Arthur* but this only increased their financial difficulties. Moreover the absence of rival companies reduced the number of new plays and therefore one of the tried methods of attracting spectators. The death of two popular actors in 1692 did not help. Matters came to a head in 1695 when the doyen of the stage, Thomas Betterton[21], secured a licence for a new company and with fifteen of the best actors and actresses moved out to the tennis court in Lincoln's Inn Fields. This had originally housed the Duke's Company before the Dorset Garden theatre was built and though it had reverted to use as a tennis court it was easily fitted up again. It was nothing like as big as the two purpose-built theatres and was poorly equipped for staging spectacles. It had however most of the notable actors and actresses and they took their following with them. Moreover, intense rivalry between the companies produced a crop of new plays, including Congreve's *Love for Love* as the opener for the new playhouse at Lincoln's Inn Fields. Conditions for both companies continued to be precarious and it is not surprising that during these last years of the century the regular actors were to be found performing at the London Fairs during the summer vacation. At the same time both theatres began to introduce displays by rope-dancers and tumblers that were more appropriate to the fair booths.

This was only one of the ways in which managers were responding to the contemporary demand for variety on the stage. Apart from operas, singing and dancing items between the acts of a play became more dominant and foreign performers and singers could earn considerably more than the actors themselves. A celebrated French dancing master was said to have earned four hundred guineas in five weeks in London in 1699. The basic salary of senior actors was only £4 or £5 a week though an occasional benefit night or a command performance at Court could increase this. The growth of music in the theatre is discussed in chapter 4 and it is enough to note here that it was a response to the competition of the concert hall and the demand for variety within one evening's entertainment. There is a revealing comment on the taste of the audience in the preface to a play produced at Lincoln's Inn Fields in 1698. The author, Pierre Motteux, apologises for the absence in his *Beauty in Distress* of 'All the things that now recommend a play most to the Liking of the Many. For it has no Singing, no Dancing, no Mixture of Comedy, no Mirth, no change of Scene, no rich Dresses, no Show, no Rants, no Similes, no Battle, no Killing on the stage, no Ghost, no Prodigy.' The audience of the 1690s, like that of any age, went to the theatre to be entertained and the companies could not afford to ignore their likes and dislikes. Prologues and epilogues played an important part in wooing the public. Prologues were more than mere introductions to a particular play and were considered on their own merits. They gave their authors an opportunity to display their wit and discuss their views on drama and other playwrights. Dryden especially used the prologue in this way for dramatic criticism. Above all, the prologue and epilogue appealed to the audience

on an intimate level, as friend speaking to friend, fostering a sense of partnership in the theatre. The audience's role as patron became more significant at the end of the century as the number of professional writers
increased. The courtier-poet of Charles II's time gave way to the independent dramatist, the writer under contract to one of the companies or to
the actor–playwright. Since the dramatist's chief income from a play came
from the profits on the third night (and sometimes the sixth) the response
of the audience was crucial. Both author and actors benefited from a
successful run, though in the seventeenth century this meant six or nine
days rather than the weeks or months we would expect today. The enormous success of Farquhar's *Constant Couple*[22] in the winter of 1699
with its fifty performances in five months was wholly exceptional. The
audience of the 1690s was drawn from a slightly wider section of society
than it had been under Charles II but it was still very small considering

22. A scene from Farquhar's *The Constant Couple*

the total population of the capital. Predominantly upper class, there were also some lawyers, men of letters, citizens and gentlemen outside the fashionable circle of the Court. One contemporary noticed an increased number of foreigners and even suggested that their lack of English had encouraged the introduction of 'Sound and Show'. Colley Cibber, the actor, referred to 'the City, the Inns of Court and the Middle part of the Town' as the chief supporters of the theatre at this time. Of course the price of seats put the playhouse out of reach of most people. Boxes were normally four shillings, the pit two shillings and six pence, and even the upper gallery one shilling. Greater affluence among the middle classes and the pull of the capital for visitors did not widen the theatre audience as much as might have been expected. The reason lies in the strong opposition to the playhouse on moral grounds. In the eyes of many people it was depraved and depraving and they shunned it.

The introduction of women onto the stage at the Restoration had helped to strengthen this antagonism. They were usually women of easy virtue (though doubtless no more so than the men) and their presence fostered the writing of comedies with a lighthearted approach to sexual morals. It is not easy to imagine the scenes between witty lovers with boy-actors on the stage. Women of course played many other roles and by the 1690s there were several actresses of considerable talent. Mrs Barry was noted for her tragic heroines, Mrs Leigh for the humour of 'superannuated Beauties' like Congreve's Lady Wishfort, and the younger Mrs Bracegirdle[23] delighted her audiences with a range of parts which included Millamant and Vanbrugh's Belinda. Unlike the other two she could also sing. Of the men Thomas Betterton was pre-eminent. He had first appeared on the stage in 1660 at the age of twenty-five so that he was sixty when he led the revolt against the patentees. His powers were still at their height and to Colley Cibber, writing forty years later, were unmatched by any other actor. This opinion was univers-ally shared. We are told that nearly all the print shops in London stocked the mezzotint of Betterton[21]. Noisy spectators were hushed by his en-trance onto the stage and eyes rivetted on his majestic figure. He excelled in tragedy but was by no means restricted to this. He made a splendid Falstaff and was equally good as a witty gallant. It is difficult not to believe that Betterton was an actor of genius. Supporting him were several others of great ability. Edward Kynaston was best known as a serious actor and James Nokes and Cave Underhill for their parts in comedy. Sandford established such a reputation as a stage villain that it was impossible to cast him differently. Each of these, and Betterton too, influenced the

23. Mrs Bracegirdle in *The Indian Queen*

playwrights, who frequently wrote parts with particular actors or actresses in mind, and by the end of the seventeenth century there was a repertoire of stock characters who appear again and again in both tragedy and comedy. This was one of the reasons why the theatre of the 1690s exhibited such close links with the earlier Restoration period and appeared to be so isolated from real life.

The actors who were able to make a living on the London stage were only a handful. There were about twenty-five or thirty in each company and during the years of the union the opportunities were halved. Even then, wages were only paid when the playhouses were open and were often in arrears. Only one or two of the leading actors shared in the profits, when there were any, of the united company and it is significant that in Betterton's new company at Lincoln's Inn Fields the shares were divided among the actors and, for the first time, Mrs Barry and Mrs Bracegirdle were put on an equal footing with the men. The sharing of responsibility for the management of the company was a bid for status as well as for financial control. Actors were regarded as servants and by many people as disreputable. The singer or musician might also be a servant but he was a respectable one and the opportunities for rewards were greater. However, if the established actors of the Theatre Royal or Lincoln's Inn Fields had to contend with insecurity and public disapproval their provincial counterparts were still more precariously placed.

Outside London there were several companies of strolling players who were licensed to act by the Master of the Revels or the Lord Chamberlain or by letters patent from the Sovereign. This latter method continued the older practice of granting a nobleman the right to keep a group of players as part of his household and at the end of the seventeenth century the best known were the Duke of Norfolk's Servants and the Duke of Grafton's. There was some competition between these two companies in East Anglia and though both performed regularly in Norwich itself the Duke of Norfolk's players seem to have ousted their rivals from the best dates in the city's social diary. Norwich had established a mini winter season for those who could not afford to go to London. Families of the country gentry, clergy and well-to-do farmers joined those of the urban élite for a round of assemblies, entertainments and promenades. There was no permanent theatre building and the players usually staged their performances in the Angel Inn. Plays were also a feature of the summer Assize week and the celebration of mayor-making in June. Apart from regular commitments in Norwich the players visited many towns in East Anglia, acting in town halls, warehouses or barns, or temporary booths. Evidence of strolling players in the West of England is scanty before the early years of the eighteenth century. The Duke of Grafton's company was active in Bristol in 1704 and 1705 and played in Bath's first purpose-built theatre of 1705. We know that Salisbury corporation banned all players in 1706 from performing in that city after listening to complaints that they corrupted the young and encouraged disorders. It seems reasonable to assume that strolling players were known there in the previous decade. Probably they included some of the smaller, less organised, troupes who scraped a living from their shows in fairs and other places. There was a great gulf between these itinerant players and the company under a nobleman's wing who might even act before the sovereign as the Duke of Grafton's Servants did at Windsor about 1706.

Information about the plays performed by the strollers is also scarce before the eighteenth century. Novelty however seems to have had the same appeal as in London and the description 'as performed at the Theatre Royal' was likely to attract an audience. Elaborate spectacles of course were difficult to copy. It is no wonder that a production of the opera *The Prophetess* staged by the Duke of Norfolk's Servants in Norwich in 1700 was received 'with great Applause, being the first that ever was attempted out of London'. The tastes of the London audience became the taste of its provincial counterparts. Only in York was there anything like an independent development. There was a plan in the 1680s to bring plays or drolls up to York from the south but that is the only reference to players before 1705 when a Mr Gilbert and his company rented the Merchant Taylors Hall for twenty shillings a week. This company later produced dramatists within its own ranks and their plays were acted in York and its neighbourhood. This eighteenth-century development is less surprising when it is remembered that York had its own intellectual and artistic circle in the late seventeenth century (see p. 104). There does not seem to have been anything quite like it in Norwich despite its larger size. Perhaps the greater distance of York from the capital accounts for the difference.

As we have seen the Norwich audience for one of the regular companies was drawn from the ranks of the affluent. Provincial audiences were not as aristocratic as those at the Theatre Royal in London but they did not extend very far down the social scale. The nearest approach to drama that the majority of people experienced was a puppet show or droll at a local fair. Fairs were beginning to lose something of their commercial role as regular retail trade increased but this did not lessen their popularity for social gatherings. They attracted every kind of itinerant pedlar, showman and player. (See also p. 95.) The greatest fairs lasted for a couple of weeks and made it worth while erecting quite substantial booths for dramatic performances[25]. They also followed each other in succession: Bartholomew Fair at the end of August, Southwark Fair from the second week in September and Stourbridge, the most important of them all, from 18 September to 1 October. So the strollers went from one to the next and to some of the lesser fairs as well. Until the end of the seventeenth century the actors of the patent theatres kept aloof from the London fairs and their drolls and puppet shows. In about 1698, however, some of them seized the chance to earn something during the summer vacation when the theatres were closed. They did not attempt to displace the type of traditional droll but introduced new ones that must have threatened to draw custom away from other booths. The drolls were only an hour long, with repetitions throughout the day. Many of them were satirical pieces on topical questions; others were based on folk tales or biblical stories. They had no literary merit; all depended on the performer as Ned Ward noted of a droll in Bartholomew Fair in 1699. 'There was nothing in the part itself but what was purely owing to his own gesture, for it was comedian only, and not the poet that rendered the character diverting.' However these drolls and the puppet shows which were based on similar themes represented an important element in popular culture. They were not debased versions from the theatres but genuine folk drama with its own stock of traditional characters. Where the Restoration dramatist might draw on the classical scene or the contemporary world of fashion the puppet play kept alive both the traditional stories of Robin Hood and of Genesis and the popular fear of popery. *The Creation of the World*, *Dives and Lazarus, The Queen of Sheba* are examples of well-known puppet plays that continued to be shown throughout the eighteenth century. So too were *Dick Whittington* and *Friar Bacon and Friar Bungay*. Punch had made his appearance in Charles II's time and by 1700 was still being billed under his Italian name of Punchinello. He was grafted on to the native tradition of clowning seen in characters like John Bumpkin or Merry Andrew and one of Laroon's illustrations of London street figures shows a Merry Andrew with Punch's hunchback and hooked nose. Though the puppet show drew nothing as yet from the content of contemporary drama (it was to do so later in the eighteenth century with burlesques based on operas) it had begun in the late seventeenth century to embellish the action with scenery and machines[24]. These were the fair's equivalent of the lavish spectacles at Dorset Garden. They were even called 'operas'. The puppets were probably marionettes and if John Harris's booth at Bartholomew Fair was not exceptional 'as large as children two years old'. Puppet shows were possibly more important than the drolls in keeping traditional folk tales alive. They were cheaper than performances by the strolling players and must therefore have reached a wider section of the public. Lucky children, too, like Sir Thomas Browne's grandson in Norwich might have puppets of their own. This heritage of popular drama was closely linked to the folk arts of the ballad and the woodcut, for the same themes are common to them all.

The players and puppeteers at a fair were under the same pressure as the managers of the theatres to compete for custom. Not only were they rivals between themselves but there were many other booths trying to catch the public's attention. There were rope-dancers, acrobats and conjurors, exhibitors of freaks and animals and waxworks, as well as the

24. Powell's puppet stage showing elaborate scenery

booths for refreshments. The fan illustrated[25] shows Bartholomew Fair at a slightly later date but the various ways of attracting custom had not changed. The booths themselves were wooden structures with a front gallery and on this cramped space actors or clowns were to be seen enticing people to the next performance. Trumpets were also blown to attract attention. There were large painted backcloths advertising the show with a picture as well as its title and the name of the proprietor. Hand bills

25. Bartholomew Fair *c.* 1721

were displayed near the doors into the booths. In this cut-throat competition for trade the arrival of the London actors must have been very unwelcome. There is some evidence, however, that the London players attracted a higher quality clientele and the better standard of their shows may have brought custom to other entertainers as well. The regular actors were also exploring other possibilities during the summer closure. According to Colley Cibber the company at Drury Lane went down to Bath in 1703 and entertained Queen Anne, and a few years later one of the same company started a regular summer season at Greenwich. It was only common sense to follow the fashionable out of the capital and it gave the young actors left behind a chance to mount plays on their own.

As we have seen the rivalry of the two companies after 1695 forced the managers to stage expensive operas, bring in foreign singers and dancers and even acrobats. It also produced a crop of new plays. In the

1695–6 season there were twenty five, and twenty in each of the next two years. Among them were the plays of Congreve and Vanbrugh which make this decade so memorable in the history of English drama.

William Congreve was only twenty-one when his first comedy, *The Old Bachelor*, was performed in 1693. It was an immediate success and ran for over fourteen nights. Congreve had been brought up in Ireland, educated, like Swift, at Kilkenny School and Trinity College, Dublin. When his grandfather died and his parents inherited the family estate in Staffordshire he was able to move to London and to enter the Middle Temple in 1691. More significantly he became a member of the group of young aspiring writers who gathered at Will's coffee house under the aegis of Dryden, and by the end of that year he had become a friend of the poet. *The Old Bachelor* was a joyously witty play but *Love for Love* (1695) was still more accomplished in its treatment of plot and characters. The comedy is full of humour and gaiety and there is greater variety in the comic characters than there was in the earlier play. Not surprisingly it was a rollicking success and gave a splendid start to the new venture at Lincoln's Inn Fields. Congreve tried his hand at tragedy, too, but luckily the popular success of *The Mourning Bride* did not lure him away from his true path or we should be without the best of Restoration comedies. *The Way of the World* was produced in 1700, a masterpiece of gentle satire on the customs of polite society. Congreve recognised that the theatre is not real life and though all the world may be a stage the stage is decidedly not all the world. The art of a play is to encapsulate the essence of some aspect of human society not just a slice of the ordinary. So Congreve suggested that natural folly on the stage was not funny at all: it was pathetic. Comedy which was based on satire was far more subtle. The refinement of his approach was lost on an audience who could not distinguish, as he said, between the character of a Witwoud and a Truewit. The play had only a moderate reception but remains the finest example of Restoration comedy with its witty dialogue and finely drawn characters. Emotion is banished; the appeal is wholly to the intellect. So we are not disturbed by the underlying immorality and the intrigues become a game of skill as contrived as marquetry. We know this is not the real world and can laugh without becoming emotionally involved.

Vanbrugh's first play appeared at Drury Lane in 1696. *The Relapse, or Virtue in Danger* was written in six weeks when he was over thirty to repay a debt to the patentee of the Theatre Royal. It was a sequel to Cibber's *Love's Last Shift* and enabled Cibber himself to score a further stage success as Sir Novelty Fashion, now Lord Foppington, described

26. Colley Cibber as Lord Foppington in *The Relapse* by Vanbrugh

as 'a Man whom Nature has made no Fool' but 'who is very industrious to pass for an Ass'[26]. *The Relapse* was well received and still more so was *The Provok'd Wife* in 1697. This had been partly written while Vanbrugh was a prisoner in the Bastille in 1692 and was now given to Betterton's company at Lincoln's Inn Fields. It therefore had the benefit of the more experienced actors and was launched on its long history of popu-

69

larity. Vanbrugh's plays take the same idealised segment of upper-class life as Congreve's and ridicule its social customs. They have the idiom of the comedy of manners where wit is the yardstick and the plot is subordinate to brilliant conversation. *The Provok'd Wife* however lacks the subtlety of Congreve's language and characterisation and relies more heavily on the idiom of stage surprises. It is beautifully engineered from the moment the quarrel is declared between the monstrously ill-matched pair. 'You married me for Love' says Lady Brute, 'And you me for Money' replies Sir John Brute who complains savagely that his two-year-old marriage has 'debaucht my five senses'. Though emotion is still absent, feelings are allowed to intrude. There is a hint here that the purely intellectual comedy of manners of Congreve is being undermined. However it is only a hint because *The Provok'd Wife* still puts intrigue for its own sake at the centre of the play. It still leaves the situation of an incongruous marriage unresolved at the end despite the mutual pardons and acknowledgements of faults. Brutality, which the main character personifies, is never allowed to erupt as something real and violent nor is sensuality given the slightest encouragement, save perhaps in the scene between Mademoiselle and Sir John Brute's servant, Razor. Vanbrugh himself declared that he had no other design in his plays than to make men laugh, 'to divert (if possible) some part of their Spleen, in spite of their Wives and their Taxes'. Vanbrugh had no more didactic aim than Congreve whose prologue to the *Way of the World* contained the author's undertaking 'He'll not instruct, lest it should give offence.'

One other playwright in the manners tradition needs to be mentioned: George Farquhar, another product of Trinity College, Dublin. His best comedies, *The Recruiting Officer* and *The Beaux Strategem*, were not written till Queen Anne's reign. His first effort, *Love and a Bottle*, was, like Congreve's earliest play, produced at the age of twenty-one but it does not bear comparison with *The Old Bachelor*. His second play, performed at Drury Lane in 1699, *The Constant Couple, or, A Trip to the Jubilee*[22], was a more competent piece. It was well constructed and amusing in its characters and dialogue and in the Congreve style. As noted earlier, it was extremely popular in its first year. Farquhar suggested he had neither 'displeased the Ladies nor offended the Clergy' by producing a comedy that was free of 'Smut and Profaneness'. This seems an unwarranted claim: *The Constant Couple* was no worse but certainly no better in this respect than other Restoration comedies. Its success on the stage can be attributed to good acting but more likely to the amusing characters that Farquhar created.

These fine comedies of Vanbrugh and Farquhar and above all of Congreve, were only a handful of the plays written in the 1690s. Most of the rest are best forgotten but there were one or two which deserve a mention and which illustrate the changes affecting the theatre at this time. In tragedy, which was almost as popular as comedy, there was a shift away from the heroic drama. The two plays of Thomas Southerne, *The Fatal Marriage* and *Oroonoko*, introduce a sentimental and pathetic note. They were both based on novels by Mrs Aphra Behn and *Oroonoko* brings an early example of the noble savage onto the stage. This same movement towards sentimentalism can be seen in Colley Cibber's comedy, *Love's Last Shift*. The invasion of feeling was fatal to the art of pure intellectual comedy and the temper of the time favoured Cibber against Congreve. The increase of farce, too, was helping to destroy the comedy of wit. Punch and Scaramouch and Harlequin were by now familiar to the theatre as well as the fair booths. While farce and sentimentalism were undermining comedy all true drama was being threatened by the increase of music and dancing on the stage and in particular by opera (see p. 80). Dryden, who had been the great figure of the Restoration theatre, wrote five pieces after 1689, two of them dramatic operas. He was, as ever, responsive to the audience of the time and understood the growing appetite for variety. This can be illustrated by his comments on the comic sub-plot in a tragedy: 'The English will not bear a thorow Tragedy; but are pleas'd, that it shou'd be lightned with Under-Parts of Mirth.'

These changes in the theatre of the late seventeenth century must be set alongside Collier's famous attack on the stage in 1698 with the publication of his *Short View of the Immorality and Profaneness of the English Stage*. Dryden, Congreve and Vanbrugh were among those particularly singled out for censure. Collier condemned the playwrights for their profane language and abuse of the clergy, for their bawdy scenes and open encouragement of immorality. He expressed in a forceful way what many people had been thinking: that the reformation of the stage was long overdue. The impact of the book was enormous. The theatre was put on the defensive and prologue after prologue reveals how sensitive their authors had become to the widespread demand for reformation. Vanbrugh felt obliged to substitute for the scene in *The Provok'd Wife* where Sir John Brute appeared in a priest's gown one in which he dressed up in his wife's clothes (a change which in fact increases the comedy of the situation). His published retort to Collier, moreover, proved no answer at all. The weight of opinion was all on Collier's side. Even before his

27. John Dryden by Kneller

book was printed the House of Commons addressed the King on the pro-faneness of the playhouses and in May 1698 a complaint was made before the Middlesex Justices that the playhouses were nurseries of blasphemy and debauchery. The year before, the Lord Chamberlain had ordered the deletion of 'obscenityes and other scandalous matters' from plays before the grant of a licence. It seems that the licensing system was now being used to censor or attempt to censor scurrilous dialogue as well as seditious sentiments. Hitherto restrictions had been imposed for political reasons but the pressure from the anti-stage opposition and the absence of any strong royal support for the playhouses, as they had had under Charles II, made the theatre more vulnerable. There were also signs that the strolling players were suffering from the general antagonism. The City of London authorities were concerned over the disorders at Bartholomew Fair and in 1700 tried to stifle the increase in theatrical performances by forbidding booths for stage plays. At Stourbridge Fair the following year the manager of the Duke of Norfolk's players was gaoled and his booth demolished for failing to obtain the sanction of the Vice-Chancellor of Cambridge University as well as that of the Mayor and Corporation.

The reaction against Restoration comedy was part of a larger movement in society for moral reform. Societies for the reformation of manners were founded during the 1690s to tackle drunkenness and vice and sabbath-breaking, and from this sprang a social concern for the poor and unprivileged. The Society for the Promotion of Christian Knowledge led to the charity school movement at home and to missionary work among negroes in the colonies. Equally significant was the tone of the new journalism. Motteux in an early issue of *The Gentleman's Journal* in 1692 poked fun at the young spark who was only interested in bawdiness, and in doing so looked forward to the world of Addison and Steele.

Drama was the dominant literary form in the 1690s as it had been since the Restoration. It was not a decade notable for poetry, though some of Dryden's last poems should be mentioned, and there was no other work of imaginative literature that can stand comparison with the best comedies. Yet the reign of William and Mary was important in establishing new patterns in literary patronage and journalism. Without an understanding of these it is impossible to appreciate the new developments in literature in the early eighteenth century that gave us Defoe's novels and Addison's essays.

Towards the end of his active life Dryden's interests shifted from the contemporary theatre to the classical world, even though he wrote several plays during this period. As a Catholic he lost his post as Poet Laureate in 1689 and in an old age of poverty and sickness his writing was his livelihood. His verse translation of Virgil's *Aeneid* is a great English poem rather than a perfect translation of the Latin, for Dryden believed that a translator must infuse his own spirit into the words or they were doomed to deadness. He continued translating in this free way and the Fables of 1700 contain some original tales as well as translations from Homer,

Boccaccio and Chaucer. Dryden was sixty-nine when he completed this last work, his inventive powers undiminished. 'Thoughts', he said, 'come crowding in so fast upon me, that my only Difficulty is to chuse or to reject; to run them into Verse or to give them the other Harmony of Prose.'

Dryden knew the value of a clear prose style and did much to encourage its use. So did John Locke who consciously wrote his *Essay Concerning Human Understanding* in a simple style in order to reach 'all sorts of Readers'. By the end of the seventeenth century English prose had been transformed. The ornate and unwieldy constructions of an older generation had given way to a plain style that is recognisably modern to our ears. Once again the influence of France is apparent. Dryden and his contemporaries admired the clarity of French prose and adopted it for themselves. The Royal Society had encouraged plainness of speech and preachers proved its advantages from the pulpit. Above all, the new English prose was the journalist's tool and it is journalism that makes the 1690s a literary watershed. During this decade four important writers of the early eighteenth century began their careers: Swift and Defoe, Steele and Addison. They were all journalists (though much else besides) and as such understood that the public, their readers, had become their new patrons. With the growth of newspapers, literary journals and a range of cheaper books it is possible to speak of a new middle-class readership which was now influencing the market. In fact an organised literary market in London had come into being.

The individual nobleman could still offer patronage to some aspiring writers with tutorships for his sons or the gift of a living, and there were government pensions or places to be had for a few lucky men like Addison, but the device of publishing books by subscription was well established by the 1690s. Dryden's Virgil of 1697 brought in the large sum of £1200 from the backers of the venture. Subscribers were sought by circulating a prospectus but alongside this publishing role the booksellers printed advertisements and lists of their books for sale and held auctions of gentlemen's libraries. While the luxury end of the market was served with sumptuous volumes such as the Tonson edition of Milton's *Paradise Lost*[43] the less affluent were provided with pocket editions of well-known authors and cheap manuals on practical subjects or books on religion or popular knowledge.

This expansion at the cheaper end of the market was matched by the beginnings of periodical literature. Most ventures failed after two or three issues and only rarely did a periodical last over several years. The successful ones managed to establish a bond between author and reader that carried through from one issue to the next. *The Athenian Mercury* which began in 1690 used the device of readers' queries. It had questions and answers on a wide range of topics, scientific, literary and philosophical. *The Gentleman's Journal*, which can claim to be the first English literary magazine, also used this method of maintaining its readership. Ned Ward, in the monthly *London Spy*, adopted the familiar figure of the country cousin being shown the sights of the capital with the serial technique of a continuous journey. His racy prose and the amusing caricatures of Londoners that his readers could recognise made *The London Spy* an immediate success. It did not have the literary merit of its successors, *The Tatler* and *The Spectator*, but set the fashion for reissuing the parts of a popular journal in book form. Ned Ward belonged to the increasing number of pamphleteers, journalists and hack writers who lived by their pens. He was outshone by Defoe but Ward helped to create a new kind of literature, part fiction, part commentary, that took the everyday world for its 'copy'. It can be compared with the beginnings of the movement in the theatre that led to the domestic dramas of the eighteenth century. Though life for writers was precarious in late seventeenth-century London, opportunities were much greater than they had been, and one of the reasons for this was the end of censorship.

Until 1695, when the Licensing Act lapsed, no printed matter could be published without a licence from the Lord Chancellor or the Archbishop of Canterbury or one of the Secretaries of State. Printing presses were only allowed in London, Oxford and Cambridge (when William landed in the West he brought his own printing press with him) and the total number of master-printers was restricted. In addition, all books had to be entered in Stationers' Hall. This censorship was enforced through an official, the Surveyor of Imprimery, who had wide powers of search and many prosecutions were made against printers and authors. The system of censorship had been in abeyance for several years at the time of the Popish Plot, which accounts for the great number of controversial pamphlets of that period. So the lifting of restrictions in 1695 was not unprecedented. The abolition of censorship was considered by Parliament not as a victory for a free press but rather as an attack on the monopoly of the Stationers' Company. However, the result was a dramatic growth in the number of newspapers and the setting up of printing presses in many provincial towns. In London *The Postman, The Post-Boy* and *The Flying Post* were all started in 1695 and published three times a week. The first daily began in 1702. Printers had quickly migrated to the provinces. In April of 1695 a William Bonny had petitioned the Common Council of Bristol for permission to establish a printing-house in the city and the following year another printer moved to Shrewsbury. Norwich probably had the first newspaper outside the capital, in 1701, and was closely followed by Bristol, Exeter and Shrewsbury. There was still one important brake on political writers: the oppressive law on libel, which was construed by some judges to include any criticism of the government. In other fields, particularly that of religious literature, this did not apply. Plays, of course, as we have seen, were subject to the Lord Chamberlain's licence and this censorship continued to modern times.

Music

In the England of the 1690s music could be heard everywhere: in house and palace, in the street, at fairs and festivals, in taverns, in churches and cathedrals, in concert room and theatre. Of course there was a wide gulf between the songs of a country inn and a Purcell sonata. Ragged psalm-singing was far from the perfection of the Chapel Royal. Yet music was ubiquitous in a way that painting and sculpture were not. It touched more people's lives than architecture, for a tune spreads more rapidly than a style of building. A good voice is a free gift: it costs nothing to use it, and there are no brushes or paint to buy. At this level of natural ability music has always been a part of human life and its social activities. At a sophisticated level the type of music produced and the standard reached depend on more complex factors: the kind of society, its cultural traditions, the means of patronage, its contact with new musical forms. The 1690s decade was crucial here. It established a pattern of musical patronage that remained virtually unchanged for the next two centuries. The public concert had arrived to stay. The Court lost its predominance as the centre of musical patronage. Opera, like drama, had to seek precarious public support in contrast to many European countries where kings or princes financed its growth. Ecclesiastical music slid into a backwater, isolated from the main stream of musical development.

Dominating the scene was one of the greatest composers England has produced, Henry Purcell[28]. His genius ranged over the whole field of music, giving us ceremonial odes like the great 1692 *Ode to St Cecilia*, sacred music like the *Te Deum and Jubilate in D* and dramatic operas like *Dido and Aeneas*. There were other composers of great talent (Blow was even Purcell's superior in compositions for the organ) but the early death of Purcell in 1695 cut short the development of an English tradition and without Purcell the rest could not carry it forward. As in the theatre, the music of the 1690s saw a flowering of achievement that had no successor. But whereas Congreve's comedy of manners was a final flourish that could have had no further natural growth, Purcell's music was still in its early summer prime and it is possible that, had he lived, English opera might have grown sufficiently powerful to withstand the Italian invasion and to have grafted its strain on to English stock. As it was, Italian opera was victorious overnight in the early eighteenth century but, imposed from outside, was always an alien art-form and failed to establish itself as part of the English cultural scene. Baroque decorative painting suffered the same fate in the end though it was popular for a very much longer time.

Italian influence had long been felt by English musicians but the new music with its emphasis on expressing emotion and hence on the soloist, and particularly the solo singer, did not displace the traditional consort and madrigal until the second half of the seventeenth century. This is not surprising when it is remembered that English Jacobean music was highly regarded in Europe and that English musicians were still in demand on the continent at the time of the Protectorate. By the 1690s however there was little interest in the older traditional music (beyond nostalgic regret). Henry Playford, the music publisher, found himself overstocked with unwanted Elizabethan works and began to sell them off in cheap lots: 'Fifty of Mr Farmers first consort of Musick in 4 parts, at 2s a set' was one entry in his catalogue. Italian singers were all the rage and highly paid for their performances, and Italian violinists were able to make a living in London without difficulty. Young men on the Grand Tour brought violins back from Italy and denuded the land, according to the contemporary Roger North. Italian opera had its enthusiasts but until the reign of Anne made little headway in England against the part-sung operas that were increasingly produced. It is, however, significant that a contemporary English translation of a Cavalli opera has recently been discovered; and we know that Evelyn saw an Italian opera in music in 1673, the 'first seen in England of this kind'. Purcell himself recommended English musicians to study the Italian composers, and it is possible that he was referring to opera when he wrote of 'the power of the Italian notes or the elegancy of their compositions'. This makes it all the more tragic that Purcell did not live to develop his own version of a fully-sung English opera, as he might have done. Addison might then have had no reason to complain as he did in 1711 that 'we are transported with anything that is not English'.

28. Henry Purcell

In his own work Purcell had absorbed the style of the new music without losing his inheritance from the English madrigalists. He drew inspiration also from popular ballads and in return put many a new tune into ballad repertory. The expressiveness of his melodies gives us a clue to that quality of human understanding and sympathy found in his greatest works of dramatic composition. Scattered throughout his works for the theatre and in a host of songs are hundreds of marvellous tunes. But his range was very wide: he produced music of the highest order for every kind of occasion, sacred or secular. Like an architect, his output was highly functional. He produced works that were a direct response to the demands of his society whether they were official compositions for the Crown, anthems and service settings in his capacity as the organist of Westminster Abbey, or incidental music for the theatre. But, as with a great architect like Wren, his art was not confined by its functional character. Just as the fifty-two City churches display a glorious variety of treatment despite the restrictions of each site and the liturgical demands that dictated certain aspects of the interiors (see p. 127), so too was Purcell able to rise above the restrictions inherent in composing for the seventeenth-century theatre. Purcell wrote pieces for over forty plays but in none of them was he more than a contributor. At best, in the operatic works, he shared in an equal partnership, as a sculptor and painter shared in the decoration of a baroque interior. Yet together these overtures, songs, choruses and dances comprise a notable group. Among them are the three operatic works that were composed within three or four years: Nahum Tate's *Dido and Aeneas* in 1689, Dryden's *King Arthur* in 1691 and *The Fairy Queen* in 1692. The last of these is a set of interpolated masques within parts of the spoken dialogue based on Shakespeare's *Midsummer Night's Dream*: there is no relation between the characters of the play and those of the masques. The singers of the latter are personifications of virtues such as Honour and Liberty – far removed from ordinary mortals. Scenic effects formed an important element of the production. *Dido and Aeneas* had greater unity (and no spoken dialogue) but with its masques was still far from the Italianate opera. It is one of Purcell's masterpieces and fairly often performed today. *King Arthur* is less familiar but is full of delightful music.

Purcell wrote very little sacred music after 1688 though some of that little is important (The Funeral Anthem for Queen Mary and the *Te Deum and Jubilate in D*, for example). His own interests drew him into the world of the theatre but this was also an indication of the changing pattern of musical patronage. The Chapel Royal and the Court ceased to be the centre of musical life in London that they had been in the reign of Charles II: stimulus came rather from the challenge of stage and concert platform. The theatre, as we have seen, in trying to attract audiences, turned increasingly from straight plays to more elaborate

DELICIÆ MUSICÆ:

BEING, A

Collection of the newest and best SONGS,

With the Additional Musick to the *Indian Queen*,
by Mr. *Daniel Purcell*, as it is now Acted at His
Majesties Theatre. Most of the Songs being within the Compass of the *Flute*.

WITH

A Thorow-Bass, for the *Theorbo-Lute*,
Bass-Viol, *Harpsichord*, or *Organ*.

Composed by several of the Best Masters.

The First Book of the Second Volume.

F. H. van Hove. Sculp.

LONDON,

Printed by *J. Heptinstall*, for *Henry Playford* at his Shop in the *Temple-
Change*, *Fleetstreet*, and for *John Church*, Sold by *Daniel Dring* at the *Harrow* and
Crown at the corner of *Cliffords-Inn-Lane* in *Fleetstreet*. And also Sold at *Oxford*
by *Francis Dollife* Book-binder, who Sells all other Musick-Books. 1696.

Price One Shilling.

29. Title page of one of Henry Playford's collections of songs

affairs, with stage machines and scenery and with more and more music. After 1695 the rivalry of the two companies stepped up the competition. Operas of the English type offered spectacular entertainment which included instrumental music, dance and song in a framework of spoken dialogue and luxurious sets. Ordinary plays, too, needed overtures and additional songs so the scope for a composer was wide, particularly when novelty sold the tickets and almost no play ran for more than five or six nights. Purcell of course was not the only musician to write for the stage. Fifteen different composers of theatre music have been identified, writing at the turn of the century, and their output was enormous. This included a lot of incidental music and innumerable songs[29]. Among the dances were gavottes, hornpipes and jigs, and lengthy chaconnes for stage processions. The most active composers working in the theatre after Purcell's death were his brother Daniel, John Eccles and the Moravian immigrant Gottfried Finger. It was these three, together with John Weldon, who took part in the celebrated competition in 1701 for a setting to a masque libretto by Congreve called *The Judgment of Paris*. Two hundred pounds in prizes was offered (raised by a group of patrons) and after each of the four winning versions had been given separately they were all performed again on the same night at the Dorset Garden theatre. The first prize went to the youngest competitor, John Weldon, who was only twenty-four. However, the contest was mishandled and Finger left England in resentment. John Eccles was a gifted composer, writing a great number of songs and several operas, and his work has been long underrated. He became Betterton's 'house' composer in Lincoln's Inn Fields and remained there for ten years. The only actress who could sing was Mrs Bracegirdle and many of Eccles' songs were written specially for her. Forty of his songs were included in D'Urfey's *Pills to Purge Melancholy* which was first published in 1699. Daniel Purcell worked mainly for the other company at Drury Lane, having come back to London from Oxford where he was organist at Magdalen College. Much of his operatic writing was done in association with Jeremiah Clarke, the composer of the famous Trumpet Voluntary. All the operas written after Purcell's death (there were nine full-length ones produced 1695–1701) were similar in form to *The Fairy Queen*. The most successful was *The Island Princess* which was revived nearly every season for the next thirty years but the most spectacular was undoubtedly *The World in the Moon* by Elkanah Settle with music by Daniel Purcell and Clarke. Settle was a mediocre playwright but a superb stager and not surprisingly his shows were very popular. He was ingenious, too, and his device for introducing the masques in *The World in the Moon* was a clever one, using the idea of a rehearsal of a new opera within the play itself.

Why did this burst of musical activity come to such a sudden end – as it did with the first Italian-style opera produced in London in 1705? The composers associated with the English opera of the 1690s were totally discredited. Eccles wrote an all-sung English opera in 1706 but it never reached the stage, and he left the theatre. Weldon, the triumphant winner of *The Judgment of Paris* prize, turned to church music and became organist at the Chapel Royal. Daniel Purcell faded into the background, unregarded. The promise that seemed to be brimming over in the music of the theatre was never realised. Practically nothing was composed for the stage for the next twenty years or so until *The Beggar's Opera* had its runaway success in 1728.

It was the clearest sign yet that patronage of music had moved on to a commercial basis. The public was infatuated with the Italian opera: it was new, it was better sung, it was the genuine article (or nearly!) from the country that was the goal of all art and music lovers. It was music of the kind popularised in London by visiting singers and virtuosi, and the concert-going audience, having tasted the joys of arias at York Buildings, was delighted to have a full opera at Drury Lane. The concert hall at York Buildings in the area between The Strand and the river had been erected in 1685 and a rival place at Charles Street in 1692. These were not the first concert rooms in London but the first to be purpose-built. Charles II's violinist, John Bannister, had given a few public performances in a room over a tavern in Whitefriars in the 1670s and a more regular series of concerts was started in 1677–8 by Thomas Britton, the 'small coals' merchant, in the loft of his warehouse in Clerkenwell. At first these were free but later an annual subscription was charged. They were still going in 1712 when Ralph Thoresby 'heard a noble concert of music, vocal and instrumental, the best in town'. Financing culture by subscription was firmly established by the end of the seventeenth century. It was the obvious method of enabling those of the gentry and middle classes who could not afford their own private concerts (nor had the space to hold them) to emulate the nobility who could. Musical managers were quick to take advantage of this new and expanding market. Accommodation was found in dancing schools and coffee rooms. The crucial difference from the musical entertainments in taverns, which continued to grow in popularity, was the entrance fee. So Robert King's licence in 1689 to set up 'a concert of music' included the proviso that 'none shall force their way in, without paying such dues as shall be set down'. Concert rooms were also established in the nearby resorts of Londoners – Sadler's Wells, Lambeth Wells, Richmond Wells and Islington. All these were established round some mineral spring or well and offered open-air and indoor entertainments in addition to the opportunity to drink the water. Sadler's Wells was named after a highway surveyor of Clerkenwell who discovered an old well with water containing chalybite. At Lambeth the charge for 'watering' and entertainment was three pence but the weekly concerts with about thirty instrumentalists and singers were one shilling. At Islington one of the attractions in the summer season was music for day-long dancing on Mondays and Thursdays. The new spas of Tunbridge Wells and Bath provided music for their more exclusive patrons on the same principle of subscription. Celia Fiennes found that 'the company' at Tunbridge Wells provided music in the pump room and for dancing, and at Bath music was financed in a similar way. Henry Playford, the music publisher, organised public concerts in Oxford as well as London. For Londoners advertisements of forthcoming attractions appeared frequently in the press and created that vital selling link between managers and the public that continues today.

While the newspapers played their part in the exploitation of this cultural market, far more important was the role of the music publisher. The first signs had appeared earlier in the century with the elder Playford's song book, *The English Dancing Master*, starting on its long career of successive editions. In the 1690s, however, there was a sudden increase in the number and variety of publications. Eight or nine publishers were in business, and of these John Walsh proved a serious rival to the younger Playford[29]. In 1695 Walsh began to publish cheaper primers for instruments and the voice than had been available before, and in greater variety. By 1703 his catalogue contained ninety-two items, ranging from small tutors at one shilling to sets of airs and songs, harpsichord pieces, excerpts from theatre pieces and sonatas and chamber music, costing from four to six shillings. His prices, except for the small primers, were not much different from Playford's but he exploited the method of engraving instead of using movable type and the cheaper process on pewter instead of copper. By the end of the century engraving was in general use and some very fine examples of engraved music came from the hands of Thomas Cross. In responding to the demand for printed music and anthologies of songs Walsh and the other publishers were also enlarging it. Musical publications encouraged amateur playing and concert-going. Concerts and the theatre whetted the appetite for published excerpts. Auction sales of music took their place alongside book auctions and offered bargains to collectors. The earliest that is recorded was in 1691 at Dewing's Coffee House in Popes-Head Alley near the Royal Exchange. Henry Playford also tried to attract customers by offering thirty shillings' worth of instrumental music and songs for a guinea subscription, to be issued in monthly collections. None but subscribers would benefit from these cut-price rates. Walsh launched in 1702 a monthly magazine, *The Monthly Mask of Vocal Music*, which was not only the first specialised publication of its kind but, in those early years of the periodical press when few ventures lasted more than two or three issues, ran for twenty-two years.

Closely allied to this rapid development in publishing was a growth in the number of musical-instrument makers, again responding to the expanding market, and in turn acting as a stimulus to musical entertainment in the amateur as well as the professional field, and to the demand for teachers and manuals and copies of music. Amateurs played

30. Late seventeenth-century spinet

a variety of instruments at home. Of the keyboard instruments the virginals were being ousted by the spinet[30] and harpsichord, but the bass viol was holding its own against the inroads of the violin family and many families still had their chests of viols. The lute remained a favourite, no doubt because it was a good accompaniment to the human voice[29]. Ability to play or sing was still widely regarded as an objective of education despite Locke's comment that the excessive time spent ('often in such odd company') could be more profitably employed. Outside the home there were, at least in London, many music clubs where amateurs could play or sing under the guidance of a professional, and these must have done much to popularise the newer instruments and the music being written for them. Less is known about provincial towns, but there was a St Cecilia Society at Salisbury and a weekly music club at Wells in which the moving spirit was the physician Claver Morris. It seems likely that the music meeting at Exeter Change patronised by James Brydges in 1700 was an amateur gathering of this kind rather than a public concert.

It is evident from this that there were greater opportunities for the middlemen in the music market: how about the musicians themselves? Undoubtedly there were more openings for the professional, though it must have been a precarious existence for the beginner and for many musicians throughout their lives. As in the other arts we know the success stories and not the failures, and very little about those who just scraped a living. London was of course a magnet for musicians out to make their fortune or simply to find work, and it is significant how many foreigners were attracted here. Like Dutch painters or engravers, or French designers, continental musicians came over in considerable numbers in the seventeenth century. Though there are some expressions of insular resentment against the foreigners, their presence probably stimulated the city's musical appetite and thereby expanded the opportunities for everyone. In the years after the Restoration Pepys has many references in his diary to Italian musicians, and there were large numbers of Italians, and some Germans, performing at the public concerts towards the end of the century. Virtuosity in violin playing and in singing was particularly admired and could command large payments. English virtuosi also had their share of public adulation: Blow on the organ, Shore on the trumpet, or Richard Leveridge the singer; and there was never in the 1690s a foreign take-over in the concert repertoire. Contemporary English composers provided much of this. It seems unlikely that a composer could make a living without some other source of income, though Jeremiah Clarke came close to the picture of a hack journalist in music. He wrote pieces that the publishers would print and the public would buy, but he was not in fact dependent on such output: he held posts as organist at times and wrote much sacred music as well. John Eccles turned his hand to whatever the Lincoln's Inn Fields theatre wanted but he was employed there as resident composer. Free-lance composing could only be done from the security of some post or supported by teaching. These posts were either at Court, in an aristocratic household, or in church or university – in other words the traditional sources of musical patronage. The new system of public patronage did not offer the same kind of appointment, though one or two were emerging, like the post of director of the concerts at York Buildings which was held at one time by Gottfried Finger and which became the pattern for the spa towns of the eighteenth century.

It is time to turn to those traditional patrons and examine the way in which their role was changing. How did the Court lose its pre-eminent position? In what way, if at all, did the aristocracy assume the Court's mantle? And why did the Church cease its active patronage of music?

Under Charles II the Court had been the centre of musical activity in England. The backbone of the musical establishment was the Chapel Royal with its thirty-two gentlemen, which included both clerical and lay singers and the three organists, and twelve choristers. Used both in the chapel and in other duties were the strings (the famous twenty-four violins) and wind instruments (including sackbuts, curtalls, cornetts and theorbos). The Master of the King's Musick was the overall director, and there were additional places in 'the private musick', for example, for two boys and a bass and two composers. Beyond these were the trumpeters and drummers, mainly deployed on military and ceremonial occasions, who came under the control of the Sergeant Trumpeter and the Drum Major. In all, musicians in the royal employ probably numbered about a hundred. Despite financial difficulties, and constant arrears of payment to the musicians and singers, Charles II maintained a lavish establishment and took a close interest himself in the music of his household. As we know from Pepys and Evelyn it was fashionable to visit the royal chapels (Catherine of Braganza maintained her own Catholic one) and to listen to the music as eagerly and critically as a performance in the theatre. The Chapel Royal was pre-eminent in English musical life not simply on account of the excellence of its choir: it introduced in the services the regular use of instrumental music, and especially of strings, and in this medium adopted the current European style of a solo line over a figured bass. Locke, Humfrey, Blow and Purcell produced works in the new style

31. A chorister of the Chapel Royal in 1690: William Croft aged 12

that gave the Chapel Royal a glamour equal to its earlier glories. It was a training ground for nearly all composers working at the end of the century and for most of the cathedral organists, so that its influence continued after its brilliant period came to an end. In the years after the Restoration the professional musical fraternity was a small one which found its inspiration and opportunity for exploration and invention within the framework of worship. This may seem paradoxical in the midst of Charles's pleasure-loving court but in the 1660s it could still be claimed that 'the first and Chief Use of Musick is for the Service and Praise of God, whose gift it is'. After 1688 the Chapel Royal maintained its choral services and still gave the best musical training available in the country, but the fire of inspiration was almost extinguished and it was never again the place for musical innovation.

James II, as a Catholic, took no interest in the Anglican worship and a separate establishment served the new chapel in Whitehall. Anglican services continued, however, in what became known as the Princess's Chapel, for Princess Anne, but standards declined. They dropped further after the Revolution: the number of singers was reduced and the string anthems were abandoned. The Calvinist William was no more interested in the Anglican liturgy than his Catholic father-in-law, and though Mary

32. Musicians of the Chapel Royal and Westminster Abbey
in the Coronation procession of James II

expressed concern and a new post of composer for the Chapel Royal was created (first held by Blow) the decline continued. Two far-reaching effects can be traced. The first was the displacement of the Court as the hub of musical life. The second was the permanent separation of church music from secular and its isolation from the main stream of development. Both resulted from the fact that the structure of royal musical patronage was ecclesiastical. There were of course many opportunities at Court for secular music but the Chapel Royal provided a focus that was missing in the other activities of the King's Musick. Unlike some German principalities there was no royal opera company and the fashion for vocal music was perforce exploited in the anthem. When the Chapel Royal ceased to be fashionable there was no counter-attraction within the Court for musicians. There were still balls at Court, entertainments for ambassadors, a few theatrical occasions, but neither William nor Mary had the same enthusiasm for music that Charles II had so obviously expressed. Though for considerably fewer than before, royal patronage continued to provide security for a number of musicians and the occasional official event still provoked musical celebration. Personal encouragement however and a stimulating atmosphere were lacking. The last years of Purcell's career illustrate as clearly as anything else the shift of musical interest. His later anthems are few and uninspired compared with those of the early 1680s. Only a special occasion like the death of Queen Mary could still evoke the finest sacred music. He continued to hold several appointments in the Royal Music but his interests were drawn to the theatre, to the challenge of dramatic composition, and as already noted he produced his operatic works in the last few years of his life.

In music, as in the other arts, we see then a surrender by the Crown of its position as the chief fount of patronage but, whereas in architecture and painting it was the aristocracy who now staked their claims to be equal co-patrons, in music their role is not so obvious. No one in the seventeenth century attempted to set up a musical establishment to rival the Chapel Royal and the Duke of Buckingham's band of fiddlers was a pale copy of Charles II's violins. The only eighteenth-century example was highly exceptional: the Duke of Chandos's chapel at Cannons for which Handel wrote the Chandos Anthems. The nearest step that the wealthy 2nd Duke of Bedford took in this direction, just after his return from Italy, was to employ two Italian musicians in his household, one of them the violinist Nicolo Haym, promoter of Italian opera. When he wanted music on a larger scale he engaged musicians for an evening at his London house or bespoke a special performance at one of the theatres. With his large income Bedford could afford to patronise on an extensive scale but what he was encouraging was music by free-lance artists and thereby the practice of public musical performance in the capital. The richest landowners in England had greater incomes than many German princes and their country houses could only be described as palaces, but in London, though their town houses were often magnificent, their social status was one of a group – élitist and powerful but still a group. This had a bearing on the form of their musical patronage. With the increasing number of their social emulators spending some time of the year in the capital, the London social season included more and more public entertainments. It was natural for the aristocracy to support these and so, in the case of public concerts, to share their patronage of music with a great many other people.

We must now turn to the second effect of the decline of the Chapel Royal from its pre-eminent position, namely the isolation of church music. Under Charles II the Chapel Royal had been in the forefront of musical experiment with the development of the instrumental anthem. After the Revolution the violins were banished from the regular Sunday liturgy: only 'solemn musick like a collegiate church' was required. Not only did composers find this limiting and, like Purcell, look elsewhere for their inspiration but it strengthened the opinion of those who held that there were only certain kinds of music and certain instruments appropriate to worship. The Puritans of course condemned all music in church except psalm-singing and some non-conformists believed that even this was a distraction from true worship. During the Protectorate organs had been dismantled and cathedral choirs disbanded, and though the Restoration had seen their rapid return the question of propriety of church music was still unsettled. Hence the publication in the 1690s of such titles as *Church-musick Vindicated* and *The Lawfulness and Expediency of Church-music*. During Queen Anne's reign it became accepted that 'there is a peculiar sort of Musick which ought to be consecrated for the Service of the Church ... and very different from that of *common* use'. Sober anthems and grave voluntaries on the organ were more appropriate than light, gay tunes. This widening gulf between sacred and secular music was to be gloriously bridged by Handel in his oratorios, but in music written for the liturgy other composers of the early eighteenth century became defensive and conservative. They ignored the new melodic styles and looked back to the contrapuntal forms of Gibbons and Byrd. They looked for something that was safe and respectable and, not surprisingly, produced little that was better than mediocre.

The basis of this attitude was the legacy of puritanism in the Church of England and its particular opposition to the theatre. In the 1690s, as we have seen, this came to a head with Collier's famous attack on the stage. It made particularly vulnerable the type of music heard in churches that was described as theatrical. The only way that the Church could be freed from such a taint was to ban this kind of music. There must be no confusion between the secular music of the stage and music designed to deepen worship, or people would come to a cathedral service, as one would-be reformer put it, 'rather to be entertained and diverted, than with a sence of Religion or devotion; for finding such turns and strains of music as they have been accustomed to hear at the Play-House, think it but reasonable, to make the same use of it in the Church'. Behaving with decorum was to be the mark of the new civilised world of *The Tatler* and decorum in church meant anthems that were sober and undramatic, and inevitably a little dull.

Even if the climate of opinion had been more favourable to the new style in church music few cathedrals had the resources to imitate the innovations of the Chapel Royal. Many of the cathedral organists had been trained as choristers under Cooke and Blow and might have hoped to use strings with their own choirs. There is no evidence that they did, beyond the existence in one cathedral library of a book of anthems scored for strings. Even wind instruments that had been common earlier in the seventeenth century fell into disuse and left the organ supreme. The best that cathedrals could afford was a good choir, and this was not always to be found. Standards were uneven across the country. In London, both St Paul's, after it reopened for worship in 1697, and Westminster Abbey had very good choirs, and outside the capital Salisbury and Christ Church, Oxford had high reputations for their music. The Dean of Christ Church was Henry Aldrich, an able scholar and architect as well as musician, and during his twenty years' leadership the choir thrived. (The dean, not the organist, was responsible for directing a choir and choosing the music, and this must have lessened the impact of a Chapel Royal trained organist). What sort of an instrument was the late seventeenth-century organ? It was not as powerful as its successors (the first four-manual organ was not built until 1710 and the pedal was introduced still later) but at its best achieved a brilliance and clarity that matched the music of the age and must have been a better foil for the human voice than the organ of today.

Outside the cathedral and collegiate chapels, the larger parish churches of London and a few provincial towns, organs were a rarity at the end of the seventeenth century. The dismantling work of the Interregnum had a lasting effect. Although there was an increase in organ building at this time, and Renatus Harris and Bernard Smith were making instruments of high quality, their work was confined to the London area and a few large churches outside. It was a century and more before organs were a common feature in the parish church. The organ at Tiverton was

built in 1696 and said to be the first in the huge diocese of Exeter, outside
Exeter itself, since the Commonwealth. It had taken ten years to overcome
the objections of the parishioners and even then the organ had been paid
for by voluntary contributions and not a penny from the parish rates.
Music in the parish church without an organ depended on the clerk with
his pitch-pipe, a group of singers and perhaps a miscellaneous band of
musickers in a west-end gallery. A handful of easy tunes for the metrical
psalms – six or eight were considered ample – was the normal congregation's sole acquaintance with church music and underlines in yet another
way the difference between London and the rest of the country.

Outside the Anglican Church the Dissenters condemned the organ and
some groups still refused to allow any singing during worship. John
Bunyan's congregation maintained this embargo all through his lifetime.
Elsewhere only metrical psalms were sung. It was among the non-conformists however that the first signs of a revival in congregational singing
were seen. The Baptist minister, Benjamin Keach, published a collection
of original hymns in 1691 and his congregation was the first Baptist
church to sing hymns as distinct from versions of the psalms. Isaac
Watts's hymns were a new thing altogether. They were liberated from
the restraints of mere biblical paraphrase and at their greatest present
the tenets of the Christian faith in simple yet noble verse. Watts was
under twenty when he began writing hymns though nothing was
published until 1706. Watts wrote his hymns to be sung and to be sung
in public worship. Bishop Ken's three great hymns for Morning, Evening
and Midnight, which were first printed in 1692 though written much
earlier, were meant for use in private devotions. Musically there was little
innovation. Watts wrote his hymns in well-known metres and in separate
lines for easy repetition. 'Lining-out' was the common practice in dissenting chapels as much as in Anglican churches for hymns and metrical
psalms alike. Tunes had to be familiar and therefore few in number. In
spite of these limited beginnings Watts was the founder of a movement
that was to have an enormous effect on worship.

One further area of sacred music should be mentioned: music played
or sung in the home. There was a long tradition of singing 'divine hymns'
reflecting both the popularity of domestic music-making and the importance attached to family prayers. Yet however religious people might be,
few went as far as Sir Samuel Moreland who, Evelyn tells us, in 1695
threw away his music books as being love-songs and vanity and played
then himself on his theorbo psalms and religious hymns. Most homes
had a more catholic approach to songs, and enjoyed both kinds! There

were several collections of sacred songs published after the Restoration and most of the leading composers wrote music for solos and dialogues. Playford's *Harmonia Sacra*, for example, published in 1688 and again in 1693, included pieces by Blow, Jeremiah Clarke and Purcell. The strong prejudice against hymns in public worship which were not versions of biblical passages did not apply here and so the range available was much wider. Settings of sacred texts were popular of course and some of Purcell's are very fine and deserve to be heard today as much as his theatre songs.

Parish churches lost their organs at the Interregnum but they did not lose their bells, and these must have been the loudest musical sounds to be heard anywhere. Change-ringing is peculiar to England (and where Englishmen have emigrated) and already as early as Charles I's reign had been founded a society of bell-ringers who later in the century established a record 'ring' of two thousand, one hundred and sixty changes. The effect of bells attracted composers and Purcell in his Bell Anthem was continuing a tradition of earlier musicians in instrumental music. However, the ringing of bells had a more practical purpose. Sometimes it signified the passing of a parishioner; at other times the celebration of some national or local occasion. It was with the latter that ringers with a peal of six or eight bells could produce their mathematical changes, and so bring to the consciousness of a remote Devon village, say, a victory of the fleet or the anniversary of the king's accession. The momentous events of the Revolution can be followed in the laconic entries of a churchwarden's accounts. At St Thomas's in Salisbury the bells were rung for the birth of the Prince of Wales in June 1688, then for the seven bishops, then 'when the King came to town', 'when the Prince of Orange came to town', and at William's proclamation as King. The ringers were paid ten shillings on some occasions, £1.2s on others. The bells were a constant drain on the parish rates, needing new ropes or clappers or wheels, which with payments to the ringers might easily account for a fifth of the annual expenditure. The carillon tradition of playing tunes on church bells was also followed in England but must have been unusual in Leeds since Ralph Thoresby noted in his diary on 13 May, 1703 the virtuosity of a young man who played 'several tunes very distinctly as if there had been a man to each bell'.

Like the bell-ringers, the town waits had a very practical role but, unlike the ringers, they needed some musical ability. Perhaps the humblest of professional musicians, their origin lay in the patrol of city streets and the playing of some instrument (often an hautboy) to mark the hours of the night. They gave public band performances on Sundays and holidays (what music they played is not known), played at municipal feasts and, hoping for a tip, greeted strangers on their arrival in the town. A small salary and a uniform were their official returns (Sheffield waits had twenty shillings a year) but like so many posts in seventeenth-century England it was the opportunity for other employment and rewards that made the job attractive. In London where there were eight official waits an entry fine was usual. A William Smith paid £32 for his appointment in 1704. In some towns the waits achieved quite a reputation and had their own particular tune named after them. A gavotte from Oxford and a hornpipe from York are among the dozen or so that survive.

Music in the street was by no means the preserve of the municipal waits. Street cries, ballad singers, rhythmic work-songs, music at the barber's shop – all these were familiar sounds. Dance and song were the normal way to celebrate a wedding, the traditional maypole-rearing or Whitsun-ale, and fairs were a magnet for itinerant musicians. Street vendors advertising their wares had their own distinctive cries, some of which had developed into a musical phrase from the natural rhythm of the words. This is a kind of basic folk music, bare, functional and transmitted in a traditional form. Several composers have drawn on these, including Deering at the beginning of the seventeenth century and Handel a century later. Laroon's drawings of the London criers[33, 45] are a contemporary record, and these and a collection like Pepys's one of ballads show a growing interest at the time in the largely unrecorded world of folk music and traditions.

The big fairs especially had plenty of musical entertainment: musical items at the theatre booths and singing and dancing at the booths where refreshments were served. Ned Ward in *The London Spy* noted that 'musick houses stood thick by one another' on one side of Bartholomew Fair. Customers still ate sucking pig and roast pork as they had in the days of Ben Jonson and expected to eat it to music. The drolls presented on the theatre booths were never complete without songs and dancing. Doggett and Parker for example advertised their new droll *Fryar Bacon or The Country Justice* with 'variety of Scenes, Machines, Songs and Dances'. Music could attract customers from a distance as well as offering items between scenes and keeping the onlooker's attention. Fairs must have been a great disseminator of tunes for itinerant musicians, like the strolling players, would go from fair to fair about the country. Among them the ballad-singer made his way, welcome not only for his songs but for the copies of the ballads he had for sale[10, 34].

33. 'Buy any ink, will you buy any ink,
Buy any very fine writing ink
Will you buy any ink and pen'

The ballad-singer was supposed to be licensed and, like the strolling player, could be convicted of being a 'vagabond' and hounded out of a town. The law was probably rarely enforced. The threat of vagabonds to a parish was to its poor rate; an influx of homeless destitutes was the bogey of any town or village. But the itinerant ballad-singer did not want to stay. He was a traveller by trade. His songs reflected the popular appetite for the sensational and the bizarre, for bawdy and romantic love tales, for convivial drinking. Always the ballad was a narrative, in a form easy to remember and easy to add to, but of no poetic merit. The ballad was also a medium for political propaganda (the pulpit being the only other channel of mass communication) and times of crisis such as the Popish Plot and the Revolution brought a rush of topical rhymes. It was only on occasions like these that there was any appreciable difference between licensed and unlicensed ballads appearing. The censorship was political, not moral, concerned with the security of the state and not the

34. Broadsheet ballad of *Daniel Cooper*

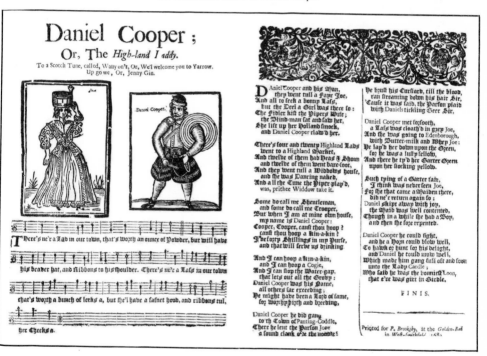

depravity of the individual. No one of course censored the tunes. It has been estimated that there must have been about a thousand broadside ballad tunes composed in the late-sixteenth and seventeenth centuries, the great age of the broadside ballad. Of these over four hundred have surivived. The common practice was for new words to be written to a familiar tune. So *Daniel Cooper or The High-land Laddy*[34] was set to several alternative tunes. A later ballad *The Crafty Barber of Deptford* was written to the tune of 'Daniel Cooper' but there seems to have been no direct connection of this tune with the ballad of the same name. At the end of the seventeenth century there were two interesting developments in the printed broadside ballad. The first was the occasional appearance of lines of music either in place of the woodcut or as an addition to it (though the musical notation is often unintelligible as in the corrupt score in *Daniel Cooper*) and the second is the increasing use of such directions as 'to a pleasant new Play-house tune'. Both are related to the popularity of theatre songs and to the output of new ones. The commercial exploitation of stage tunes in published collections of songs[29] spread into this cruder section of the market. Some three dozen street ballads used Henry Purcell's tune 'If love's a sweet passion' from *The Fairy Queen*. 'Jenny Gin', one of the tunes suggested for *Daniel Cooper*, originated as a song in Mrs Aphra Behn's play *The City Heiress*. Very often, however, it is not possible to discover which new play-house tune is inferred, though for the singers the ballad metre was usually an easy one which would fit a number of tunes.

The most famous ballad tune of the late seventeenth century was 'Lillibulero' and it has of course survived to play an active role in the twentieth century. The tune is first found in 1686, with no title, in the second edition of Robert Carr's *The Delightful Companion*. No one knows who composed it. Purcell's name has been linked with it because he produced an arrangement of 'A new Irish Tune' for virginals or harpsichord in 1689. The original ballad which used the tune was a satirical attack on Richard Talbot, the Earl of Tyrconnel, who became Deputy of Ireland in February 1687, written either on his first visit or on his second in the following year. From this time onwards the tune was linked irrevocably with the Revolution and the Protestant Succession. The first printed copy of the ballad appeared in December 1688 but it was already familiar in the south-west by the time William landed at Torbay. In a verse broadside printed at Exeter on 5 November entitled *An Epistle to Mr Dryden* were the lines

> 'Dryden, thy Wit has Catterwauld too long
> Now Lero, Lero, is the only Song.'

According to Bishop Burnet, the whole army and then everyone in city and country alike 'were singing it perpetually'. Could this have been the 'common ballad' with strong Protestant associations that the organist at Gloucester Cathedral played on Thanksgiving Day in 1688 after the morning service 'to the great scandal of religion, profanation of the Church, and grievous offence of all good Christians'? Moreover, reprimand failed to stop him repeating the offence after evensong. It was certainly the tune that Thoresby's young man played on the bells a few years later, and it was used in many ballads and songs and ballad operas of the eighteenth century.

The story of 'Lillibulero' illustrates the part that popular music could play in the life of seventeenth-century society. Originating almost certainly from the pen of a professional musician, the tune was taken up by a satirical ballad writer and because it responded to the mood of so many Englishmen, caught the popular imagination. No other art-form could have spread so quickly through the country: a tune, and in this case, a catchy refrain, was not restricted to the literate, though the sale of ballad broadsheets reinforced the oral transmission and, with the chapbooks, was the only printed and illustrated material to reach the mass of the people. The large number of copies of broadsheet ballads that have survived is an indication of their widespread appeal. The enormous number of different ballads that are known to have existed underlines the vigorous nature of this particular folk art. As an indication of the variety available at any one time, one London publisher in 1689 had over three hundred ballads in stock. But beyond that the ballad tradition was so firmly implanted that its adaptation in the ballad operas of the 1720s and 1730s was an instant success. A tune has always passed easily from folk music to the world of sophisticated composition and back again, but here the ballad form itself was adopted, an indication of the strength of its roots in English society.

Painting and Graphic Arts

Every branch of the pictorial arts was dominated by foreigners: Kneller and Dahl in portraiture, Verrio and Laguerre in decorative painting, the Van de Veldes in marine and Sieberechts in landscape painting. The best flower painters were Monnoyer and Bogdani, the best sporting painter Jan Wyck. Knyff and Kip led the field in topography. England in the later seventeenth century was a land of opportunity for continental artists. Not only did the Court and aristocracy positively encourage foreign tastes but increasing wealth among the commercial classes greatly expanded the market for works of art. At the same time conditions in Europe favoured the flow across the Channel. Economic decline in Holland reduced opportunities for her large number of artists and persecution of the Huguenots in France brought a stream of refugees to England. Evelyn writing in 1699 believed that it was only in 'face-painting' that Englishmen had made their mark. Portraiture alone offered financial return for those 'greedy of getting present money for their work'. On the surface Evelyn was right. There was no established native tradition in landscape or genre painting. Yet beneath the top layer of foreign artists practising in England we can see the forerunners of the great eighteenth-century achievement. Only in decorative painting was there no native development. This is not to dispute Thornhill's success (he was the greatest English 'history' painter) but it was success in an alien style. When the Palladian tide turned against the vast wall and ceiling paintings of the baroque palaces it was a phase that simply came to an end. In other areas of pictorial art, however, the signs of future development are there and we must now look at the wide and delightful variety of art being produced.

There was an ever increasing demand for portraits at the end of the seventeenth century. It had always been fashionable for the wealthy, but now the prosperous merchant was equally determined to hang his family on the walls of his house. It is significant that it was through a merchant called Banckes that Kneller received his introduction to London. By contrast, the only way that the foreign decorative painters could get established was by royal or aristocratic patronage. Kneller quickly acquired the position of leading portrait painter after Lely's death and maintained an enormous output for forty years. Like Lely before him, his studio was something of a factory, with a regular tariff for portraits; a full-length, for example, was £50. Rarely was the whole picture done by the master himself. Assistants, whose names are known, painted the background, the draperies, the wigs – everything except the face. It has been suggested that the Kit-Kat size of portrait, which comes half way between the head and the three-quarter length portrait, and of which the Dryden[27] was one of the first examples, was adopted by Kneller for practical reasons. He could paint the portrait from a life-size drawing of the sitter's head without having to scale it down, and thus speed up the production process. There is such a quantity of surviving Kneller-type portraits of mediocre worth that the quality of Kneller's own work has been submerged. Some of his finest portraits belong to the reign of William and Mary. The study of Sir Isaac Newton, for example, is conventional in the pose and the oval frame but this cannot subdue his individuality and intelligence. There is a striking and elegant portrait of Matthew Prior in Trinity College, Cambridge, and a fine double painting of the Duchess of Marlborough playing cards with Lady Fitzhardinge. The portrait of Dryden (also in Trinity College) which was painted towards the end of the poet's long life (c. 1698) is a masterpiece. The Court Painter has dropped the artificial mould and left us with a supremely sensitive study. Here we have a man completely at ease, his hand resting as lightly on the laurel wreath as his loose robe hangs from his shoulders. The colours are restricted to a range of grey and silver.

Beyond these examples of Kneller's sensitive response to interesting sitters there were the more formal parade portraits, represented here[35] by the full-length of Margaret, Countess of Ranelagh. This was one of the set of eight Hampton Court Beauties painted for Queen Mary and hung in her Water Gallery. They were much admired at the time and for many years after. Kneller is still better known for another set of portraits, the Kit-Kat Club series, now in the National Portrait Gallery. Over a period of about twenty years Kneller painted more than forty members of the club who presented the portraits to the secretary, Jacob Tonson the publisher. Though the project only got under way in 1702 or so the

35. Margaret, Countess of Ranelagh, by Kneller

36. Michael Dahl, self-portrait

club itself began earlier, as is shown by the survival of a bill for the wine
consumed at one of its gatherings in 1689 (with gallons of claret, canary
and other wines listed). It was a dining and toasting club of eminent
Whigs whose interests ranged from politics to literature and the arts, and
whose members included Kneller himself, Vanbrugh, Congreve, Steele
and Addison. Not only did these writers and artists meet the great Whig
magnates as equals but this exclusive and influential group encouraged

the patronage of artists along party lines. This was less marked in the 1690s than it became in the next reign and, as we have seen, did not at first determine the kind of art sponsored. It was also a clear sign that circles outside the Court were asserting their role in artistic patronage.

Kneller had only one rival, the Swedish Michael Dahl, but he was a lesser painter altogether. His Petworth Beauties, for example, are an insipid crew. They are portraits of peeresses commissioned by the Duke of Somerset in the late 1690s, but are not nearly as effective as their Hampton Court rivals. His self-portrait of 1691[36] in the National Portrait Gallery, however, is in quite another class. Dahl was also Kneller's rival in political alignment for he was in the Tory Earl of Oxford's artistic circle.

Among the considerable number of other portrait painters known to have been at work in the last ten years of the seventeenth century only a few produced canvases of any quality. But the very existence of so many who could make a living from painting is significant. Still more is the fact that a number of provincial towns including York, Oxford and Exeter could support a resident painter. This growth of artistic patronage in the provinces is matched by the start of local presses after the lapse of the Licensing Act. London never lost its cultural hegemony but there now developed these small urban circles of artistic and literary interests. They were usually strengthened by sympathetic local landowners and were nearly always dependent on London links. York perhaps was less so than other provincial capitals (see p. 64) but even there the interesting group of local virtuosi that included five Fellows of the Royal Society used its London correspondents to secure books or artists' colours. This group of friends met at the house of Henry Gyles, the glasspainter, and included physicians and antiquaries, an architect, writers and artists. Francis Place was one of them and his interests ranged from etching and mezzotint to experiments with stoneware (see p. 186). During the next century the growth of urban centres and particularly the spas of Tunbridge Wells and Bath encouraged this kind of cultural pattern but it began before the end of the seventeenth century.

Some provincial painters were hardly more than craftsmen ready to turn their brushes to anything. They would paint woodwork or shop signs, coaches or coats of arms, an overmantel or a complete room. It seems likely that, except in London, it was only the portrait painter who could afford to specialise. The successful portrait painter was obviously in a different category from the jobbing decorator, and as we have seen could rise to high social position. Kneller was knighted by William III and built himself a large country house (now Kneller Hall, the home of the Royal School of Military Music): he had a London house and kept a coach and six. The jobbing decorator was clearly an artisan, learning his trade through apprenticeship to a master-craftsman. But what of the many practitioners who came between the two extremes? How many were 'artists'? In particular, the dividing line between the craftsman and the professional artist was at its haziest in the area of interior design. When did the covering of woodwork or other surface with a protective layer become a creative process? When it was skilfully 'marbled', when it was painted in a pattern of flowers or only when its design was an allegorical or historical subject? In the late seventeenth century financial reward for mural painting, and the social status that went with it, depended on nationality. No English painter was paid as much as Charles II's foreign decorative artists, Verrio and Laguerre, and it was exceedingly hard for English painters to get important commissions. Only with Thornhill's success at Greenwich in Anne's reign was a major undertaking won by an Englishman. Even then, calculation of payment was made according to the footage of ceiling to be painted, a method used alike for carved cornices or painted walls.

Like the fashionable portrait painter, the decorative painter who was commissioned to paint a room or a great staircase did not expect to complete it without assistance. Verrio's entourage at Burghley where he was working for the Earl of Exeter during the 1690s included two painters to help with the figures, a specialist on architectural painting, a gilder, besides his two sons and at least one other assistant. Beyond this kind of teamwork the full-blown baroque interior was a collaboration across the arts. Architect, painter, sculptor and carver worked together to produce a unified artistic creation. Verrio's Heaven Room at Burghley or Laguerre's state rooms at Chatsworth are splendid examples of the grand baroque interior. The Chatsworth chapel[15] is also beautiful.

Though there were as many as fifty staircases painted in this grand manner in the last quarter of the seventeenth century, most patrons could not afford such lavish decoration. Oval pictures inserted in elaborate plasterwork, a conservative practice in the 1690s, provided a cheaper alternative. Walls might be marbled or panelled with inserted decoration. Many of the grand interiors are faded and dirty today so that it is difficult to appreciate what their impact would have been when freshly painted. Nevertheless, many are also exceedingly dull and it is a relief to turn to one of the most enchanting interiors that has survived. A set of painted panels (of 1696) by Robert Robinson once decorated a room of a house

37. Part of a panelled room painted by Robert Robinson

in Botolph Lane, London, and they have been re-erected in the boardroom of Sir John Cass's School in Aldgate[37]. They are charming scenes of life in some remote imagined continent, with pagodas that clearly represent the East and feathered princesses that seem to float out of some Inca kingdom in the West, but mixed with gondolas and architectural scenes that indicate Venice, tobacco slaves from Virginia and strange, delightful birds and beasts and fishes. Maybe, as Mr Croft-Murray suggests, the paintings were done for an East India merchant and the intention of the artist was to waft him away from the cares of a hard-headed business to an ethereal land of fantasy. Such an interest in the exotic – and the primitive life – was not new. John White's drawings of Virginia, Hollar's engravings of people of the Old and New Worlds, Aphra Behn's novel *Oroonoko*, had all fed this curiosity. Chinese imports, especially decorated cabinets, wallpaper and porcelain, were arriving in increasing quantities and chinoiserie designs were being used on English furniture, textiles and silver. There is, in the Victoria and Albert Museum, another set of painted panels by Robinson which are more markedly Chinese, though with the same feeling of fantasy.

The fashion for chinoiseries stemmed from a curiosity about the East that did not go more than skin-deep and was happily transformed into decorative devices. The interest in topography, on the other hand, represented an urge for accuracy and a desire to make an exact record. It reflected the contemporary interest in scientific classification. Leonard Knyff's drawings of palaces and houses which were engraved by Kip for his *Britannia Illustrata* (1707–8) were all drawn on the spot and represent the exact lay-out of house and grounds, and Kip engraved others as well[54]. They have great documentary interest and are attractive records, but without the imaginative touch of some of Sieberechts' views. Jan Sieberechts was trained in the Low Countries and only came to England in his forties, so his painting retained its Flemish character. His views of English houses bridge the divide between topographical record and landscape. The house is accurately drawn but the distance melts into a very soft light and this sense of distance anticipates English landscape painting of the eighteenth century. Examples of Sieberechts' work in the 1690s include the huge painting of Wollaton Hall and the charming prospect of Henley-on-Thames. Francis Place, the amateur artist who has already been mentioned in connection with the York group, also foreshadowed the English landscape school with his pen and wash drawings of the Yorkshire countryside. The *Dropping Well, Knaresborough*[38] has a touch of romanticism that is far removed from a Knyff bird's-eye view. Landscape painting verged into topographical art on one side and into decorative painting on the other. It was fashionable to have the panels in the carved overdoors filled with a 'landskip' and to regard them as part of the general decoration of a room. Alternative subjects were a seascape or flowers and in the hands of the Van de Veldes or Monnoyer or Bogdani the quality was high. With lesser artists the painting was correspondingly poorer but occasionally we are attracted by the very naivety of a provincial example. The panel picture, on wood or canvas, was a form of decoration that the less wealthy could afford.

Decorative painting in its highest reaches was intensely dramatic, with the illusionism of the baroque style. It also had a direct link with the

38. Francis Place: pen and wash drawing of *The Dropping Well, Knaresborough* (32 cm × 40 cm)

theatre, for the elaborate scenery offered opportunities for painters like Robert Robinson. He contracted in 1700 with Elkanah Settle to paint 'severall sets of scenes and Machines for a new Opera' within seven weeks. Since the price was fixed at £130 he must havè found scene painting very lucrative compared with other commissions. None of these stage sets of course has survived and though we know that they were spectacular we do not know what they actually looked like.

The theatre offered visual splendour for a few hours at a time, and since the sets were re-used they could dazzle (or bore) again and again. The real ephemeral art of the decorative painter was to be found in the public pageants. Royal coronations, marriages or funerals, celebrations of treaties, all offered an opportunity for display. The Revolution made little difference here. A constitutional monarch had as much need of publicising himself as the most autocratic king, and William might have gained more popularity if he had been willing to repeat the one progress through the country that he undertook. In London the royal processions were extravagantly staged. Distinguished artists were commissioned for such pieces as the temporary triumphal arches. The only rival show was the annual Lord Mayor's Pageant. Perhaps it underlines the powerful position of the City in national affairs that the Lord Mayor's Shows at this time were particularly elaborate. The part deviser of these, Elkanah Settle, has already been mentioned in connection with the theatre and we know the names of some of the painters he employed. A William Thompson, for example, was responsible for painting the barge of the Clothworkers' Company in 1695. These pageants were, like the great baroque interiors, a co-operative achievement. Dramatists, actors (for what else were the participants?), painters, carvers and wax modellists combined to produce a spectacle of popular art. Perhaps art for the people would be a more accurate description as the subject matter was often classical or allegorical. This was where the ordinary Londoner played his part as a patron, for it was the existence of this particular urban community that engendered this kind of display.

Apart from the shows connected with fairs the streets themselves provided a display of visual and decorative arts. By the end of the seventeenth century the permanent retail shop had established itself, though it had not ousted the temporary stall. Beyond the influence this had on the pattern of consumer buying, more objects were on view all the time. Window-gazing had begun, though there was no window-dressing as such before the nineteenth-century plate-glass revolution. Is it possible to argue that this minor social change had its part in fostering the uniformity of taste that is so marked a feature of eighteenth-century England? It did not, however, do away with the need for shop signs.

Before the streets were numbered, the only way that John Hannam, for example, could direct customers to his goldsmith's shop was to tell them to come to 'the Goulden Cup, the north side of St Paul's Churchyard beyond the Narr[o]w passage towards Cheapside'[41]. The signs hanging from iron brackets were more popular than carved panels on the walls. Some of the latter had been inserted in the new houses after the Great Fire in an attempt to keep the streets free of obstructions but they were not nearly so effective in catching the eye. Eighteenth-century pictures of London streets show more boards, too, than carved emblems[3]. However, both kinds offered good scope for the ingenious designer. An elaborate sign might be commissioned from one of the coach-painters of Long-Acre but the average tradesman was more likely to patronise one of the sign-painters. They congregated in Harp Alley, off Fleet Street, and stocked a miscellaneous selection of boards. William Steward at the King's Head sold 'signes ready painted and Bushes for Taverns, Border Cloths for shops, Constable's Staffs, Laurells for Clubs, Dyall Boards for Clocks, Sugar Loafes and Tobacco-roles'. Tobacco-rolls or twists, either on their own or under the arm of a blackamoor, were very popular as tobacconists' signs. Some of the carved Black Boys that have survived were quite small and probably stood inside the shop. The Black Boy from the Pinto Collection in the Birmingham City Museum is only sixty centimetres high[39]. His crown and kilt are tobacco leaves and he has the

39. Tobacconist's sign, carved and painted

characteristic pot-belly and short legs of seventeenth-century figures. Some signs, like the Black Boy, became closely associated with a particular trade or profession: sugar loaves with a grocer, a golden fleece with a woollen draper, a cup with a goldsmith or the three brass balls with a pawnbroker. Others were unrelated. A tradesman would continue to use the sign of the business previously carried on in the shop and might add another of his own. Very few of these early trade signs have survived and the same is true for inn signs even though they continued in use when the others were abandoned for numbers. They are now usually in museums but occasionally still on a building, as in the case of the charming board of three cherubs' heads outside St Mary Woolnoth in Lombard Street, London.

Our best contemporary evidence of what they looked like comes from trade cards and bill-heads. Some of the latter even show the bracket on which the board was hung. Of course, they are themselves examples of the engraver's art. The cards of the 1690s fall into two kinds. There are those which show some sophistication in design and execution, and are probably copper-engravings. (During the best period for trade cards, in the mid-eighteenth century, well-known artists like Bickham, Sturt and Hogarth can be found as designers.) The others have the naivety but also the vigour of popular art and are often wood-engraved. Com-

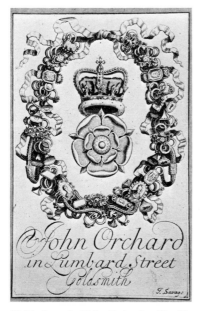

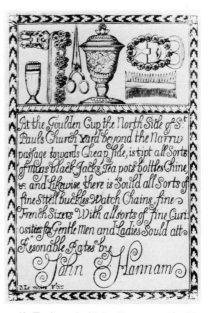

40. Trade card of John Orchard, goldsmith   41. Trade card of John Hannam, goldsmith

pare the two goldsmiths' cards illustrated here[40, 41]. Both incorporate examples of their wares but in totally different ways. On John Orchard's the rings, the miniatures and the jewels are woven into a ribboned wreath, and the Rose and Crown set sedately in the middle. The lettering of his name, street and calling is well formed. On John Hannam's card the Golden Cup is admittedly in the centre but the rest of the space has just been filled with a pictorial assortment of articles and the lettering has slipped out of line towards the end. Yet it has an endearing freshness

42. Trade card of Hugh Granger, cabinet maker

about it, and it is this quality that attracts us to the Angel of Alderman-bury[42]. It is likely that the shop sign of this cabinet maker, Hugh Granger, was in fact a carved emblem or at least had been at some earlier stage.

For many people the woodcut of the broadsheet was their only contact with pictorial art. Designs were crude and stereotyped but their visual images brought home the issues of the day. When these were illustrating a ballad with a catchy tune, their impact was enormous. Some of these ballads, like 'Lillibulero', became famous overnight; some popularised an emblem like the oak tree of Charles II or the orange tree of William III. The broadsheet woodcuts are pictorial headlines, aimed to attract and then impress a message. The sparse cut-outs like the marching soldiers in *The Female Warrior*[10] are effective because they do not attempt too much. There is no background to distract from the figures and little variation between the individual volunteers. Satirical prints are more complicated, and often crowd a series of events into one picture. But, like the cruder woodcuts, they have a political message and use the language of symbols to express it. The orange tree stands erect in the centre of the cartoon *England's Memorial*[11]. It is decorated with heraldic shields of the family of William of Orange and under it stand a stiff row of the chief characters of 1688. James's Queen holds the Child, whose birth brought a Catholic heir to the throne, and James is drawn blaming France for his troubles. Representatives of the Lords and Commons are close to the trunk of the tree which remains rigidly upright 'as safe from Hells assaults as the Laurel is from thunder'. The tottering Church of England is being saved by God's Providence working through the Prince of Orange and the stand taken by the Church itself. Again, it is the tree's symbolic shade that brings relief. The French King and his council of devils blow without avail on the branches. The Pope's Nuncio and the 'whole Heard of papists' flee from the 'deadly plant' and its smell of freedom. This print must have been circulating in the second half of 1688, and is typical of the political cartoons of the period. Each sets out to tell a story and in a pictorial language that could be understood by the ordinary Englishman. It is a long way from the classical allegories of a ceiling by Verrio or Laguerre which could only appeal to the educated. But on its own level of contemporary symbolism it was art that had some realism about it.

Most of these political engravings are anonymous. It is only for some of the more accomplished products that we know the designer or engraver. There are, for instance, some packs of historical playing cards that were almost certainly designed by Francis Barlow, the first English painter to specialise in animal and bird studies. One set of 1690 has scenes of William's invasion, a favourite subject of the time. Another contemporary set which has survived (designer unknown) has scenes of sentimental gallantry and a rhyming couplet on each card. These cards were novelties and could be bought at toyshops. They are an interesting sideline for the printer but insignificant compared with the growing market for book illustrations. The second half of the seventeenth century saw the publication of some sumptuous editions, especially of classical texts. These drew on the best illustrators available. Dryden's translation of Virgil, for instance, published in folio and quarto by the famous bookseller Jacob Tonson in 1697 was illustrated by Hollar, Faithorne and Lombart. The same publisher brought out the first illustrated edition of Milton's *Paradise Lost* in 1688 with an engraving for each of the twelve books. Medina designed all but one of these. His illustration for Book I is a splendid foil to Milton's drama[43]. The intermingled limbs and tongues of fire lead the eyes up to the magnificent figure of Satan. He stands, dominant above his crew, his face and body lit by the fire below, and his bearing that of a military leader. His Roman tunic does not seem

43. J. B. Medina's illustration to Milton's *Paradise Lost*, Book 1

incongruous, nor the classical style of the palace of Pandemonium in the background. Medina has managed to keep the vigorous outline that is found in the best of signboards but invests it with depth of meaning. His other designs for *Paradise Lost* are not as powerful but, judging by this one, it seems a pity that he painted nothing else beyond portraits.

The increase in printing and engraving during the later seventeenth century was a response to an expanding market. At one end were the wealthy collectors, at the other the purchasers of the 'sixpennies'. Cheap books like these and the even cheaper chapbooks were illustrated by crude woodcuts. They were much smaller than those on broadsheets but had the same qualities of naivety and directness. From the number of interspersed cuts and type ornaments in chapbooks they were obviously catering for a semi-literate readership. It is indeed the woodcuts that attract us today: the texts have little merit in themselves. They included all kinds of stories – legendary, historical, supernatural, religious – but so mutilated and condensed that sometimes their origins are unrecognisable. But they were a popular item in the pedlar's or chapman's pack and sold wherever he went. None of these was produced specifically for children at this time (this was a later development) but they must have been enjoyed by them. Heroes like Don Bellianis of Greece, Guy of Warwick, the Seven Champions and John Hickathrift that Steele's godson knew so well were only to be found in chapbooks.

One specialised manual should be mentioned here: the writing-master's copy-book. The expansion in trade in the second half of the seventeenth century required a corresponding increase in the number of clerks who could keep the books. New writing schools were opened, including the one at Christ's Hospital, and writing-masters like John Ayres and John Seddon preached the virtues of the round hand in a series of copy-books. These were in themselves minor works of art, beautifully engraved on copper plates. Ayres in his preface to *Tutor to Penmanship* explained that the high price (fifteen shillings) was caused by the care taken to engrave 'so nigh the Nature of the Pen'. Seddon's *Penman's Paradise* of *c.* 1695 was engraved by John Sturt and includes several examples of the fanciful flourishes made by a continuous line of the pen[44]. Similar lettering with flourishes appears on the brass memorial plates that came into fashion about this time. There are a number in the Bristol region that coincide with the establishment of the brass industry there.

Apart from engravings and woodcuts in books, the book or print seller sold prints on their own. The range was wide. There were reproductions

115

44. The penman's flourish: a plate from Seddon's *Penman's Paradise*

of portraits and of well-known paintings; views of foreign parts and topographical prints of English towns and buildings; prints of contemporary
events such as the coronation of William and Mary or the Queen's
funeral procession; engravings of birds, flowers and animals; maps in increasing variety. Ladies still bought prints to serve as copies for their
amateur efforts at home, just as Mrs Pepys had done in the 1660s. There
is a revealing glimpse of this aspect of the print seller's business in a letter
from Pierce Tempest, the publisher, to Francis Place in 1686: 'the ladys
have solely left painting Mezzotintos yet they doe sell a little especially
fancy's Heads & bawdy soe I am provideing 3 or four new ones Against
the Terme 2 Queens a new Confession 2 Fancys after Laroone ...'. The

45. Street figure from Laroon's *Cryes of London*

interest in scenes of ordinary life was growing, fed by painters like Laroon and Heemskerck and soon to come into its own with Hogarth in the eighteenth century. It is yet another indication of the widening circles

117

of interest in the arts. Laroon's *Cryes of the City of London*, published by Pierce Tempest, are far removed from any courtly patronage of art[33, 45]. They were still, of course, an outsider's view, a polite version of the street vendors. But now there was a market for such pictures. Ordinary Londoners, not exotic Indians, had become appropriate subjects for the artist. Similarly, the number of art collectors was increased by the invention of the mezzotint. A portrait in oils was still the privilege of the wealthy but an engraving made with the new mezzotint technique could offer a substitute that had artistic merit of its own. The new process was seldom used for book illustrations because it lost its quality with repeated impressions but for reproducing paintings it was unrivalled. The mezzotint of Kneller's Betterton is a fine example[21].

Mezzotinting was also unsuitable for maps and for these line engraving continued to be used. London still lagged behind Amsterdam and Paris as a centre of geographical science but some notable contributions made at this time foreshadowed England's leading role in the eighteenth century. Halley's magnetic charts of the Atlantic and then of the World were of immense benefit to navigation. Captain Greenvile Collins's survey of the coasts of Great Britain did not bring him the international fame of Halley but it was the first complete Pilot Book in English of the British coastline and the volume of forty-seven charts and silhouettes was reprinted throughout the next century. On land, the most original cartographer was John Ogilby whose survey of the roads of England and Wales in a continuous strip form was the ancestor of a whole family of road books. His *Britannia*, first issued in 1675, was republished in 1698 and the importance of inserting roads in county maps was recognised and soon became established practice. Robert Morden incorporated some of Ogilby's material in his series of county maps for Gibson's edition of Camden's *Britannia* (1695) and also drew on Greenvile Collins for some of the coastal counties. His maps were not based on an original survey: they were a compilation of available material, with a serious attempt to modernise spellings. Artistically they rely on an elegant lay-out and a single ornamental feature, the cartouche with the name of the county[46]. Was Morden anxious that decoration should not interfere with the informative purpose of the maps? Or was it a deliberate rejection of the tradition of map engravers as Palladian purists later rejected the architecture of Vanbrugh and Hawksmoor? Highly elaborate maps continued to be made in the eighteenth century so that Morden's example did not set a new fashion. Greenvile Collins's charts showed a more typical approach to decoration. There were ships of all sizes in the sea and the cartouches

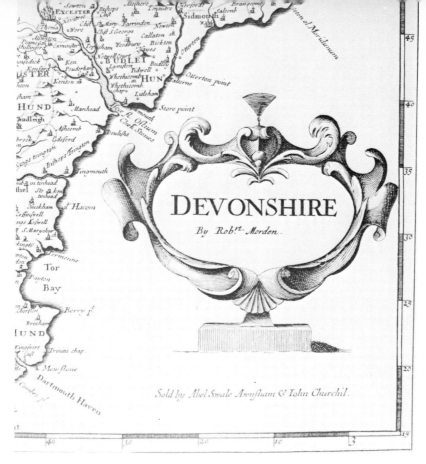

46. Robert Morden: cartouche and part of map of Devonshire

were pictorial. The same style can be found in heraldic arms and in book-plates, and is closely related to the cartouche monument in stone. (See also ill. 42.)

Such similarity in graphic design is natural. What the increase of engravings in the late seventeenth century showed, too, was the role of the print in spreading knowledge of styles in the other arts. Designs were copied from engravings in glasspainting, silverware and embroidery. On delft pottery they were often 'pounced', that is to say, traced from prints by rubbing pumice or charcoal through pinholes made in the engraving. The furnishing designs of Daniel Marot and the ironwork designs of Tijou became familiar through the publication of their engravings. The do-it-yourself japanner was given patterns to copy by Stalker and Parker's manual[9]. Above all, it was engravings that enabled English architects to know something of continental styles and it is to architecture that we now turn in the next chapter.

Architecture

The 1690s was an important decade in the history of English architecture. Sir Christopher Wren still dominated the scene and was engaged on some of his greatest works. St Paul's Cathedral reached the stage of being opened for worship though the dome and the western towers were not completed till the reign of Queen Anne. Much work was done on the interiors of the City churches and some of the steeples were built. There were large-scale additions to Hampton Court[47,48], and Greenwich Hos-

47. Hampton Court Palace from the air. The Tudor buildings are to the left and Wren's Fountain Court to the right. Part of the Broad Walk and the Great Fountain Garden are visible beyond the Palace

pital[7] was designed and begun. But the decade is also significant for the rivalling of royal palaces by aristocratic undertakings and, in stylistic terms, a break away from the prevalent country house pattern. The south front of Chatsworth[52] was an architectural innovation and hard on its heels came the first expression of the fully baroque style of Hawksmoor and Vanbrugh in Castle Howard[5]. While the period thus introduces a new element into English architecture it also marks the final triumph of symmetry and proportion in the smaller house, the end of the long period of transition from the Tudor vernacular style to the fully classical. The extensive amount of building activity is reflected, too, in the improvements in technique. Sash windows began to replace casements, bricks were widely used as they became cheaper, home-produced pantiles began to be made and tile-hanging appeared in south-east England. Moreover, the convenience of the corridor was recognised for the first time in the design of a large house though this innovation was long in taking hold.

In 1689 Wren had held the post of Surveyor-General for twenty years. He was nearing sixty. Behind him lay a wealth of experience, a list of notable buildings to his credit and the training of a group of highly skilled craftsmen at the Royal Works. It is hard to remember that he was completely self-taught, that his first essay in designing a Cambridge chapel was as a professor of astronomy. His first-hand knowledge of contemporary architecture in Europe was restricted to a single visit to Paris in the 1660s: for the rest he was dependent on prints and architectural treatises. Nor did he gain from the stimulus of any other architect of his calibre. The assurance with which he approached the undertakings of the 1690s came from his own inventiveness and the experience gained from putting his ideas into practice. The fifty-two City churches rebuilt after the Great Fire of London hold a special place in this regard. In the variety of design and the ingenuity with which he solved their practical problems they form a vital stepping-stone to St Paul's. But these churches were by no means his only concern. St Paul's itself was a major commitment throughout these years and there were many other projects that claimed his attention. The beautiful Library of Trinity College, Cambridge, showed his mastery of a completely Italianate style, Tom Tower in Oxford, on the other hand, his respect for his Gothic predecessors, and the Royal Observatory at Greenwich a somewhat impish delight in the fantastical which links him with the folly-builders of the eighteenth century. In Chelsea Hospital and Charles II's new palace at Winchester Wren began to experiment with the spatial arrangement of large blocks.

In both of these he was given the chance to build entirely new buildings without the need to adapt to earlier ones on the site. Greenwich Hospital is the fruit of this experience in large-scale planning.

Wren's first projects of the new reign, however, were at Hampton Court and Kensington. Whitehall was too close to the river for William's asthma and neither he nor Mary liked the Palace. It was very different from their favourite houses in Holland and plans were quickly afoot for enlarging the early seventeenth-century house at Kensington and transforming the Tudor palace at Hampton Court. At Kensington there were successive additions which offered little scope to the architect: the Clock Court to the west is on a pleasant domestic scale with two storeys and dormer windows above and the exterior remains today much as it must have been in Wren's time. The later King's Gallery employs giant pilasters in brick to give it a more imposing appearance and is probably the work of Nicholas Hawksmoor who was Clerk of the Works at Kensington. Hampton Court, on the other hand, gave Wren far greater opportunity. His first scheme proposed the pulling down of the old Tudor buildings except for the Great Hall and the construction of a vast new palace, in a style more exuberant than the earlier project at Winchester, and aligned with Charles II's Long Water to the east and a great chestnut avenue in Bushey Park to the north. The design finally adopted was considerably smaller in scale, less costly and far less destructive of the existing buildings. As so often in his career Wren was forced to compromise, abandoning his Grand Front and the basic concept of an axial plan for a range of buildings round a court on the Park side of the Palace. This was still aligned with the Canal and Wren's original design for the gardens on this side was carried over into the compromise scheme, and remains today largely the same. A great parterre of box scrolls was laid out on Charles II's semi-circle between the East Front and the Long Water and smaller canals constructed to mark its edge and the line of the Broad Walk. It was enriched with thirteen fountains, splendid wrought-iron gates and many garden ornaments. A few of these have survived, including Nost's lead sculptures on the gateposts at the end of the Broad Walk[64] and Tijou's magnificent screen and gates which can still be seen at the bottom of the Privy Garden[81]. George London was responsible for laying out the gardens but it was to Wren's design as part of his overall plan for a suitably majestic setting of the Palace. Few formal gardens of the period have survived so we are fortunate to have the shape of Hampton Court if not all the ornaments and planted parterres.

Today the visitor enters the Palace under the Tudor Gatehouse and walks through the two Tudor courts little prepared for the completely different character of Wren's range of buildings round Fountain Court. But he has no doubt of the integral relationship between the East Front[48] and the Park: each gains from the other. The East Front is

48. Hampton Court Palace: centre part of the East Front, facing the Park

the major façade but the South Front is treated in a similar way as befitted the range for the King's Apartments. They were designed as a whole and expected to be seen as such. What has been achieved? It is a satisfying building without being a beautiful one. It has dignity and poise but its static character makes it a little unexciting. In its own terms, however, it makes a powerful impact. Strong horizontal lines balance the verticals of each set of windows. These are differently shaped on each storey – round-headed on the ground floor, tall and rectangular on the main floor, circular on the second and square at the attic level above the stone horizontal band. The repetition of this window pattern and the overall flatness of the façade would be monotonous but for the contrast of brick and stone, the central feature on each front and the slight projection of the end bays on the South Front. Variation on the surfaces comes, too, from the carved detail. The keystones on the windows and the frieze on the East Front repay a closer look and there is a fine relief in the pediment above the Park entrance by Caius Gabriel Cibber. This portrays Hercules overcoming Superstition, Tyranny and Fury, and was a compliment to William III, glorifying his struggle against France. The symbolism is echoed in the decoration of the Fountain Court. There are lion-skins, carved by William Emmett, round the circular windows and grisaille paintings of the Labours of Hercules by Laguerre. Inside the Palace the martial allegory is taken further in Verrio's painting of the King's Staircase. The decoration of the interior was not begun till 1698 and we might never have had Wren's superb suite of rooms if fire had not destroyed Whitehall Palace. On Mary's death in 1694 William lost heart in the enterprise and work was stopped. He only renewed interest after the fire and Wren was then able to bring in craftsmen to complete the building. There are ceilings by Verrio, carvings by Gibbons, metalwork by Tijou. The very high standard of craftsmanship throughout reflects the attention that Wren paid to detail and the understanding that existed between the architect and his team of artists. Drawings exist, for instance, to show how Wren designed the outline on a large scale and handed over to Gibbons

The Whitehall fire destroyed everything except Inigo Jones's Banqueting House; it seemed at last that complete rebuilding might be possible after a century of abortive plans and piecemeal alterations. But Wren's plan of a great new palace remained a dream: there was no money forthcoming, and in any case William was uninterested. We have to turn to Greenwich to see how Wren's continuing concern with the problems of spatial planning was translated into reality.

Greenwich from the river is one of the most beautiful architectural sights in England[7]. Here, as elsewhere, there were existing buildings to be considered: the Queen's House by Inigo Jones and Webb's King Charles's Block. Wren had hoped to give his open courtyard, which incorporated the second of these, an imposing centre-piece but this would have blocked the view of the Thames from the Queen's House. Instead the eye is arrested by the two domed towers set in from the riverside blocks and the sense of movement from one to the other is increased by the contrast of light and shade. The paired columns of the colonnades play a major role in this (as well as leading the eye back to the Queen's House) but are helped by the niches under the pediments and the arrangement of the columns round the drums of the domes. Though other archi-

124

49. St Paul's Cathedral from the south

tects were involved at Greenwich and the work stretched over a long period, Wren was responsible for the idea of the courtyard open to the river and the design of its essential elements – Hall, Chapel, domes and colonnades. Its serenity and its harmonious form leave an unforgettable impression of beauty that is only matched by St Paul's. These two buildings entitle Wren to be considered an architect of European stature.

St Paul's occupied Wren during the whole of his career as an architect. The foundation stone was laid in 1675 and the cathedral was finished in 1711. It cost nearly three-quarters of a million pounds which was an immense sum for the period. Even today among the tower blocks of the City its vast size is overwhelming at close quarters and even at a distance the dome is still majestic. The recent cleaning of the stonework has revealed the detail of the carving and enables us to appreciate afresh the part played by the rich surface decoration against the clean outlines of the building[49]. Inside, the removal of grime and the Victorian glass has done a like service. Much of the exterior decorative work and the fittings of the interior were completed in the 1690s when there was an increase in income from the coal tax. The main fabric of the City churches had been finished by the accession of William and Mary and since steeples and furnishings could not attract grants from the City's rebuilding fund the bulk of the coal tax went to St Paul's. By 1697 sufficient progress had been made for the Thanksgiving Service for the Peace of Ryswick to be held in the choir but no start was made on the dome or the western towers for several years. The final plans for these were not settled till about 1704. Nevertheless Wren had been continuously concerned with the problems of the dome from the very beginning, and there is evidence in the late 1690s of his shift of interest towards the baroque. St Paul's then offers us for this decade unparalleled examples of the skill of such craftsmen as Kempster, Maine, Gibbons and Tijou. It also shows us how Wren's architectural style matured as he developed an understanding of the dramatic qualities of the baroque style. It seems possible that Hawksmoor was the catalyst in this stage of Wren's development. His concern with a newer monumental style is first seen in the Writing School for Christ's Hospital (1692) and as we shall see later it flowered on a grand scale in partnership with Vanbrugh. The relationship between Wren, Hawksmoor and Vanbrugh is still unresolved despite recent research. Yet the rise of a younger generation of architects – among whom Talman must be included – does not prove that Wren's later works must be attributed elsewhere. Throughout his life Wren had absorbed ideas from outside and used them in the process of evolving his own very individual designs. There is no reason to suppose that he did not share this new interest in grandeur and three-dimensional architecture (strongly evident in the early scheme for Hampton Court). However, Wren's handling of the baroque idiom was always restrained. He shunned the extremes of fashion and wrote himself that 'an architect ought to be jealous of Novelties, in which Fancy blinds the Judgement; and to think his Judges, as well those that are to live five centuries after him, as those of his own Time'. What is clear at least is that this New Look in English architecture makes its appearance at the end of the seventeenth century and that this coincides with the emergence of Hawksmoor, Talman and Vanbrugh.

A good illustration of Wren's willingness to experiment with baroque ideas without complete surrender can be seen in a group of steeples designed in this period. Steeples, like the furnishing of the interiors of the new City churches, were the financial responsibility of each parish and apart from one or two early ones (like St Mary-le-Bow) are much later than the main fabric of the church, which included the base of the tower. As a group the steeples display even greater variety than can be found in the interiors, an astonishing range of treatment in both stone and lead. Towards the end of his life Wren wrote of the importance of spires rising above the neighbouring houses and being 'of sufficient Ornament to the Town, without a great expence for enriching the outward Walls of the Churches, in which Plainness and Duration ought principally, if not wholly, to be studied'. Unfortunately, the scale of post-war London building has deprived us of the panorama that Canaletto painted and which can be seen in the 1710 Prospect[2] but in some cases replanning has opened out the immediate setting of those that survive. The contrast between the richness of the steeples and the plainness of the walls is at once apparent (a contrast echoed in the elaborate wood carving and plain whitewashed walls of the interiors). St Bride's, Fleet Street, (1701–3) familiarly nicknamed the wedding-cake spire, is tall and consists of four octagonal storeys, diminishing in size and finishing with an octagonal pyramid[50]. It is a splendid statement of Wren's belief that an architect should be above everything 'skilled in Perspective'. Christ Church, Newgate (completed 1704) takes a different motive, the diminishing square. St Vedast, Foster Lane (built 1694–7) has alternating concave and convex features on each storey, introducing a sense of movement above the stolid tower that is the hallmark of the baroque style[51]. St Magnus Martyr, London Bridge (completed 1705) introduces a lead cupola and spire above an octagonal stage. All were indeed ornaments to the townscape of the rebuilt city. The furnishings of the interiors of Wren's churches suffered

50. St Bride, Fleet Street: steeple   51. St Vedast, Foster Lane: steeple

more severely from the bombing than the towers and steeples, and though some have been restored there has been much alteration of Wren's original arrangements. Moreover, though the 1690s saw most of these interiors 'beautified', the architectural structure which determined the shape of the interiors was already built. Nevertheless, Wren's views on the needs of Anglican worship and how his interiors provided for this are relevant to any understanding of the religious architecture of the time and apply equally to the last two decades of the seventeenth century. Churches needed plain glass windows so that there was enough light for people to read the prayerbook, the altar needed to be visible from every seat and a clergyman audible whether he was in the pulpit, at the reading desk or at the altar. Hence Wren's view that 'in our reformed religion it would seem vain to make a Parish Church larger, than that all who are present can both hear and see'.

The demands of an Anglican parish differed from those of a cathedral or an Oxford college or an aristocratic household, and still more from those of a nonconformist meeting, but beyond this factor of function there is a wide variety of styles represented in the churches and chapels built in the 1690s. This makes the decade particularly interesting as a watershed in ecclesiastical architecture and can be illustrated by a look at four completely different types: an East Anglian meeting-house, a brick parish church in Wiltshire, a Gothic Revival church in Warwickshire and the baroque chapel of the Duke of Devonshire.

Beyond St Paul's and the City churches there was, in fact, little of architectural note in religious buildings, for the chief contribution came from the nonconformists and they only required the simplest of meeting-houses. The exceptions among the latter were to be found in the prosperous towns of East Anglia or the south-west. Affluent congregations could afford to embellish their woodwork or erect a façade as richly decorated as the early eighteenth-century chapel at Frome in Somerset. Chapels such as these were self-confident statements of the Dissenters' new status in urban society but a restraint in workmanship was the more usual hallmark of the meeting-house. Moreover, the interior planning of all the meeting-houses was strictly functional, and a similar pattern is found everywhere: pews or benches, and galleries on three sides, the pulpit on the fourth, the communion table in the middle. The little meeting-house at Walpole in Suffolk, is but the vernacular rural equivalent of a sophisticated city example like Norwich Old Meeting or Friar Street, Ipswich[17]. The latter is an elegant building with its double-pitched roof, deep cornice and fine doorways with carved supports to the pediments[12]. It was built by a local master-carpenter in 1699 and exemplifies the assurance with which the provincial craftsman could now handle the classical idiom. The interior is still more remarkable. The joinery is of a high standard, with turned rails and carved detail. Defoe thought it excelled any other meeting-house he had seen, even in London. We do not know who was responsible or who in particular carved the decorations on the beautiful tulip-shaped pulpit but it must have been someone familiar with the woodwork of the City churches.

The other three buildings are all Anglican churches or chapels. Farley Church in Wiltshire was almost certainly designed by Wren. Like the almshouses nearby, the church was the gift of Sir Stephen Fox, the Treasury Commissioner, for his native village. Some of Wren's craftsmen are known to have worked on the almshouses and it is highly likely that Wren also provided the outline plan for the church. It is in brick and in a plain classical style, a style fully accepted from now on as appropriate for a church. The second is St Mary's at Warwick, rebuilt after a disastrous fire in 1694. It can be considered as the first Gothic Revival, and not Survival, church in England. It was designed by Sir William Watson, a provincial mason-architect, and built by the Smith family of masons; and while the choice of style was undoubtedly governed by the need to harmonise with the chancel which was not burnt down, yet both the tower and the nave are quite unmedieval in character. Gothic architecture was no longer a living tradition: from now on it was to be only a source of decoration for romantic designers. The third example is the Chapel at Chatsworth, noteworthy for its splendid interior[15]. As we have seen in chapter 2, only in such private chapels did the ecclesiastical baroque of the Stuart chapels survive the Revolution. No parish church in the Anglican communion would have tolerated such decoration. The private patron, on the other hand, did not exclude his chapel from the decorative treatment of his State rooms. Laguerre painted the walls with a scene of Christ healing the sick and the ceiling with the Ascension; Cibber was the sculptor of the altarpiece and Samuel Watson was responsible for the woodwork. The picture of Christ and St Thomas is by Verrio. Further details will be found in the next chapter (see p. 151).

The Earl of Devonshire (created Duke in 1694) was one of the chief promoters of the Revolution and had played a leading part in inviting William to England in 1688. Chatsworth rivalled the royal palaces in grandeur and in the standard of its rich interiors, and as such symbolised the shift of power from Crown to aristocracy. It is significant, too, that it was here that a new style in architecture emerged. The South front of Chatsworth is the monumental front of a palace[52]. It recalls an Italian palazzo or Bernini's Louvre and breaks completely away from the current type of country house with hipped roof and dormer windows. What makes it so impressive? It is firstly its massive build-up from the rusticated basement through two floors to the straight balustrade and its sculptured urns. The roof is concealed and so cannot detract from the impact of the rectangular façade. The strong horizontal line of the balustrade is countered by the giant pilasters at each end which emphasise the way these outer bays are set slightly forward. All the windows on the main floors have heavy, protruding keystones. There is nothing gentle here at all. It is palatial, not domestic. Talman has turned his back on that

52. Chatsworth House: the south front designed by Talman

comfortable, intimate scale that marks so much of English seventeenth-century architecture.

Talman was also responsible for the east front of Dyrham Park (1698) which echoes the Chatsworth design in its rectangular outline, the straight balustrade, the hidden roof and the slight projection of the outer bays. As at Chatsworth it was the garden front and not the entrance but, though still monumental, it is less decisive. The giant pilasters have gone; so have the emphatic keystones (though they reappear on the orangery windows) and the insertion of an attic floor reduces the palatial impact compared with Chatsworth. The carved eagle on the centre of the balustrade and the treatment of the door and the window above it draw attention to the centre in a way that is subtly different from the Chatsworth central feature. There the branching stairs (especially in their original form) simply reinforce the purpose of the basement, raising the upper storeys to a more impressive level.

Chatsworth and Dyrham share a further similarity: they were both built in stages to replace earlier Elizabethan houses and both involved more than one architect. At Chatsworth, the lack of a coherent design from the start was offset by rebuilding on the same courtyard plan and taking the scale from that of Talman's south front. At Dyrham, Talman was the second architect and built his new range of rooms on to the back of the earlier (1692) west front[53]. The two sides are therefore never seen

53. Dyrham Park: the west front designed by Hauduroy

together, and the continuation of orangery on the east and stable block on the west fill the south side. Though Talman's front is grander and on a larger scale a certain unity results from the similarity of the balustrade. The first stage of rebuilding at Dyrham did not produce important architectural innovation as was the case at Chatsworth, but it is significant in not being yet another of the hipped-roof, dormer-windowed houses so popular throughout the second half of the seventeenth century. Why did Dyrham's builder turn away from current fashion? Was it William Blathwayt's own idea or simply that of the architect he employed? Once again we find that England's foreign alignments by no means determined artistic fashion. William Blathwayt was William III's Secretary-at-War and his acting Secretary of State on the continent during the war against Louis XIV. But this did not impose a barrier against French culture. Blathwayt's architect was in fact a Frenchman, perhaps a Huguenot refugee, called Hauduroy. He is otherwise unknown. His design recalls a

French 'hotel' with its enclosed terrace and central balcony, and the close fenestration is like the contemporary great west front of Petworth whose French character is unmistakable.

We do not know why Blathwayt chose Hauduroy. As a man, in Evelyn's words, 'very dexterous in business' William Blathwayt may have regarded the unknown designer as a bargain. (Hauduroy complained he had only been paid £10 in all, including travelling expenses.) He may also have wished to keep the reins firmly in his own hands. Certainly he remained in close contact with the rebuilding even when campaigning with William III and the weekly accounts that he received from his bailiff were carefully annotated and returned.

Blathwayt and Dyrham illustrate perfectly the transformation of a successful civil servant into a country landowner. Blathwayt's family background was typical of those behind many seventeenth-century fortunes. His grandfather was in business as a London cutler and his father was a lawyer but he himself followed his uncle's career as a government official. He held various offices under Charles II and James II, proving himself such a valuable administrator that despite his admiration for James he was confirmed in his posts by William III. One of the greatest benefits of the Revolution being 'Bloodless' was the continuity of an efficient executive which had been growing more and more effective during the 1670s and 1680s. Blathwayt's offices brought him in a large income, and larger still in perquisites and commissions, but it was his marriage to an heiress that enabled him not merely to establish himself in a country estate but to rebuild on such a lavish scale. Today Dyrham still evokes the feel of the 1690s. Much remains unaltered though Blathwayt's collection of books and some of his best pictures have gone. Most of the panelling is intact, the Siena marbling is still visible on the walls of the cedar staircase, gilt leather hangings from The Hague still decorate the east hall and Dutch paintings the west. All over the house can be found the blue and white delftware from Holland that became so fashionable in England. There are splendid tulip pots in the shape of pagodas, jardinières and decorative urns, tableware and dishes. It is not surprising to find such a strong Dutch influence in the house considering Blathwayt's many visits to Holland with the King. Delftware, pictures and furnishings were bought in the Netherlands and shipped back to Dyrham. On the other hand, it is interesting that while the garden and its setting was unmistakably Dutch, the architecture owes nothing to Holland.

Gardens are more vulnerable than houses to decay and they have suffered more radical changes. The design of a country house cannot be properly appreciated divorced from its setting and yet how rarely does a contemporary garden survive from before the eighteenth century. The 1690s saw the final unclouded glory of the formal garden in England. Shortly afterwards the desire for something more expansive and more natural began to spread, and Pope's dictum of Nature controlled by Art was transformed into practice in the first landscaped settings of the country house. No new fashion in the arts has been so devastating to its predecessor. The formal gardens that Knyff drew and Kip engraved have been all but obliterated. The only remains of the original Dyrham gardens are the long terrace above the church (left side of the print[54] and the Neptune fountain at the top of the hill. But Kip's View shows the extent of terraces and parterres on the steep slopes of the Cotswolds, the water cascade of two hundred and twenty-four steps, the fountains and the long

54. Kip's View of Dyrham Park, showing the elaborate gardens

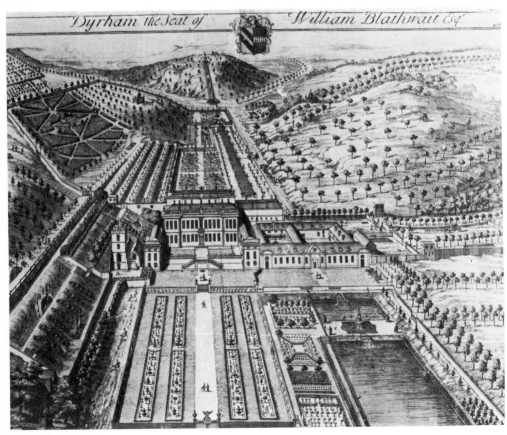

canal. Many of these were temporarily revealed by the drought of 1976. The long formal beds and walls enhanced the impact of the house and its enclosed courtyard, while the idea of enclosed space was reiterated in the rectangles of broderie and walled divisions. Garden ornaments, some lead, some stone, echoed the carvings on the house. House and garden were, then, complementary: they were intimately related in one overall design.

Intimacy is one of the hallmarks of the Dutch garden of the seventeenth century. The flatness of the land encouraged enclosures by walls or hedges so that one passed from one separate portion to another. The other essential ingredient was water: the long canal, the fountain (to give the missing dimension of height) and the reflections of clipped tree or statue. The Dyrham garden incorporated steep slopes and so its Dutch character was modified. Similarly, the Derbyshire hills gave tremendous scope to the designer of Chatsworth gardens whose great cascade can still be seen today. But at Westbury Court in Gloucestershire, in the flat lands of the Severn valley, there is a pure Dutch water garden. It is the only one of its kind in England to survive (evading the eighteenth-century land-scaper, the nineteenth-century restorer and the twentieth-century bull-dozer – just). In Gloucestershire alone twenty-eight of the fifty-eight gardens illustrated by Kip were water gardens. Today, just a few years after the National Trust's rescue and restoration, the hedging and topiary are at a stage similar to Kip's view. The pavilion has long windows typical of Holland and its height provides a vertical feature to offset the flatness of the garden. At Westbury the house and garden are not contemporary. When Maynard Colchester inherited the estate in 1694 he did not rebuild the old Elizabethan house with his wife's fortune: he spent his new wealth on the garden. The designer is unknown but it seems likely that Col-chester was influenced by a neighbour who had recently laid out new gardens and was half Dutch. These water gardens entailed considerable outlay and laborious upkeep. The more extravagant ones demanded great resources, particularly where elaborate water engineering was involved, as at Chatsworth and Dyrham, or where great sculptors and other artists were commissioned, as at Hampton Court. The reaction against the formal garden was a shift in taste but it was also a convenient economy.

The other strand in English garden design at the end of the seventeenth century was that of Le Nôtre. His wide vistas and radiating avenues were rarely adopted on the scale of Versailles or with such an addiction to sym-metry but their influence was ubiquitous. From the great avenues at Hampton Court to a modest example such as the Old Rectory garden at Inkpen the impress was the same: straight lines of trees, vistas marked with statues and natural informality clipped away with the shears. The evergreen had been popularised by Evelyn, and the yew and holly were tamed into pyramids and globes and all kinds of beasts and birds. The finest remaining topiary garden of this time is at Levens Hall, Cumbria, but the smallest garden could boast a clipped yew or two. Tender evergreens like bays and oranges, prized for their shiny leaves, needed protection in the winter. The orangery became a common feature during the reign of William and Mary and has left us with some of the most attractive buildings of the time. Nicholas Hawksmoor's orangery at Kensington Palace was built after William's death but typifies the happy combination of warmth and dignity. A passion for gardens was about the only interest William showed in his English palaces. Bentinck, who shared the King's enthusiasm and brought over special plants from his estate in Holland, became Superintendent of the Royal Gardens but the real work was done by his deputy, George London. With his partner, Henry Wise, London designed many of the grand gardens of the period, including Chatsworth, and was certainly involved in the plans at Dyrham. The artistic success of the garden depended on more than the overall design, though this was of course important. Like the house it complemented, the creation of the garden was a co-operative effort. Artists in stone, lead and wrought-iron provided ornaments that set off the geometric lines of parterre and walks; engineers manipulated the water into fountains and cascades; the skill of gardeners raised the plants, bushes and trees without which there would be no garden. The aim was to create pleasure grounds that could be enjoyed visually: statically from the house and in movement along terrace and avenue. How often did Celia Fiennes note the 'convenience' of the grand walks or the long rides through woodland when she visited country houses and delighted in the prospects they afforded. Behind the popularity of the formal garden was an expansion in the nursery business. London and Wise themselves ran a flourishing concern at Brompton. Others were sited in Shoreditch. They were examples of the kind of specialised business springing up in increasing numbers to serve the prosperous middle classes. At the same time there was growing interest in foreign plants, fed no doubt by the expansion in overseas trade. This did not affect the kind of garden in fashion but it widened the choice of plant and tree. It also stimulated the art of botanical drawing. Dutch influence here was paramount. The urge to collect and classify, however, is part of the general scientific movement of the century: collecting data on which to base a comprehensive explanation of the natural world.

It is difficult to detect any sign in the 1690s that the formal garden would soon fall out of fashion. Innovations came in the architecture of the great house but not in its setting. The formal garden seemed to suit the palaces of Vanbrugh quite as well as the designs of Wren. It was also admirably fitted for the smaller town house, indeed the smaller house anywhere. Sir William Temple, reflecting in his garden of Moor Park on the Chinese 'sharawadgi', did not reject the possibility of beauty in irregularity but felt it was difficult to make a success of it. With regular figures, however, 'its hard to make any great and remarkable faults'. He followed this cautious advice himself but more from a desire to recreate a garden he had loved in his youth.

The largest of the aristocratic palaces built in the generation after the Revolution was not begun till 1705. Blenheim, therefore, falls outside our period but all the elements of baroque extravagance and the new approach to architectural mass can be seen in Castle Howard[55]. Vanbrugh was

55. Bird's-eye view of Castle Howard

a complete amateur. He was a playwright turned architect and the only building he designed before the Earl of Carlisle accepted his plan for Castle Howard was the curious house he built for himself in Whitehall in 1699. Dramatic is the adjective that comes quickly to mind when we look at Vanbrugh's creations. Theatrical show, with its elements of illusion and surprise, is translated into stone. The illusion of depth on the stage became in fact a triumphant reality in architecture. Castle Howard does not present a two-dimensional front to the viewer: it is the third dimension of volume that makes it so distinct a development from Chatsworth or Dyrham. Vanbrugh was helped here by Hawksmoor, who, it has already been suggested, was the originator of this new feeling for mass that is first seen in England in the 1690s. During this decade Hawksmoor began to receive independent commissions, including that for Easton Neston, and was obviously taking more responsibility as Wren's assistant. Yet he always remained in subordinate posts. He was not born a gentleman like Vanbrugh, Wren and Talman, and his very professionalism may have told against him. Vanbrugh, the amateur and man of the world, took the limelight while Hawksmoor stood aside as the paid official so it is difficult to assess their relative contributions. There is no doubt, however, that Castle Howard carries the scale of aristocratic splendour to new heights. The stone hall is like the domed crossing of a great baroque church, built for ceremony and magnificence. Vanbrugh may have produced inconvenient living quarters for his patrons but works of art on this scale had one very practical result. They provided employment in the area for many years. Over two hundred men were working at Castle Howard at a time. Some craftsmen were brought down from London (the Office of Works in this way acted both as a training school and as a distributor of skills) but most were recruited locally. At Petworth, for instance, one of Wren's master masons, Samuel Fulkes, was employed as resident supervisor but it seems probable that John Selden, the superb carver, was a local craftsman. The position at Dyrham was similar. Standard work was given to local craftsmen but anything special was entrusted to specialists of standing. So John Harvey of Bath (who later built the first Pump Room there) carved the urns for the east front balustrade and the eagle, and Robert Barker from London carved the woodwork of the Balcony Room. Beyond the craftsmen there were enormous numbers of workmen involved, on foundations and levelling, on the preparation of bricks or quarrying of local stone, on cartage of all kinds of materials. The building of a great house like Chatsworth could bring prosperity for a generation to the local community. Where livelihood was usually precarious extra casual work could make all the difference between starvation and plenty, and for some there was regular employment, both skilled and unskilled. Architecture is not only the most public of all the arts: it is also the most closely associated with society, and in execution the most co-operative.

As we have seen, new trends in post-Revolution architecture appeared first in the great country house. Monumentality is the hallmark of both Talman and Vanbrugh and it is not surprising to find little of their styles in the smaller house. Right through this period and into the years of Queen Anne, the pedimented, hipped-roof type of country house remained popular. We need not be surprised. Few styles have combined better the functional needs of family life with such charming exteriors and satisfying proportions. Tadworth Court in Surrey is an excellent example[58], brick-built of two equal main storeys over a basement and with attic dormer windows in the roof. The stone dressings include the prominent quoins of the centre, and a finely carved doorway. Only the charming garlanded oval in the pediment and the scrolls above the door link this house with the baroque movement. But it is decoration *applied* to the building; it does not spring out of the house itself. Another good example is found on the well-known National Trust house in the Close at Salisbury, Mompesson House, where the decoration is similarly re-

56. Cotswold vernacular: Tetbury, Glos.   57. Classical refronting: Burford, Oxon.

stricted to the treatment of the doorway and the curving scrolls round the window above. Such decoration is also found earlier in the century, particularly on church monuments. Just as Renaissance detail was super-

58. Pedimented front and dormer windows: Tadworth Court, Surrey
59. East Anglian town house: Bury St Edmunds, Suffolk

imposed on a medieval house so was baroque ornament in seventeenth-century houses.

Tadworth Court is one of a great many houses built in northern Surrey between 1690 and 1730 in what Ian Nairn and Nikolaus Pevsner call 'the earliest wave of Suburbanisation'. Tadworth, like others, was built for a city merchant and represents the common practice of investing commercial wealth in land. A new feature, however, of London at the end of the seventeenth century was the existence of merchants or financiers who did not feel it necessary to express their status in a landed estate. (The depressed state of the land market was a factor, too, and the more attractive returns from urban investment or government stocks.) In 1695 in the centre of London was found the highest proportion of wealthy and substantial households, and this 'urban gentry' seems to have lived in style without ostentation. By the 1690s all the major buildings in the City had been rebuilt but it was a decade of beautifying the interiors – of com-

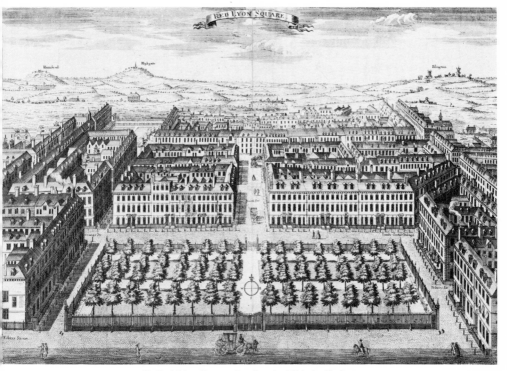

60. Red Lion Square, London, by Nicholas Barbon

pany halls and institutions as well as churches. The building boom continued to the west and north-west, with the standardised town house in
rows or squares. The greatest speculative builder was Nicholas Barbon
whose Red Lion Square[60] and neighbouring streets were composed of
identical houses. Their uniformity resulted not so much from an artistic
sense of civic planning as from the financial advantage to be gained from
large-scale operations. No square was actually planned as an architectural
whole until the development of the Grosvenor Estate in the 1720s.

London had discovered the practical advantages of the classical idiom
for the town house before the Civil War. Other cities eventually followed
suit until by the end of the century the transition to a fully classical style
was complete. Towns like Warwick and Beccles, which were both hit by
disastrous fires, were transformed by their streets of neat brick houses.
Other towns changed in more piecemeal fashion with the addition of an
individual house or two like the fine Cupola House in Bury St

141

Edmunds[59]. Virtually everywhere the new urban building was in the classical idiom. To a large extent this was also true of the country with the exception of cottages, and of farmhouses in the upland areas which were still being built in gabled style; an occasional gabled survival can even be found in the south-east, and the Cotswold gable was never ousted entirely from the region in the next two centuries[56]. At the end of the seventeenth century there were Yorkshire moorland farmhouses being built with features familiar to lowland England of the sixteenth century: stone mullioned windows, continuous string courses, four-centred door-ways and low storeys. Neither here nor in some of the Dartmoor granite and thatched long-houses was there any slavish following of symmetry, the essential element of classical design. Functional needs still came first.

The best evidence for the establishment of the classical style as the norm is perhaps to be found in the innumerable examples of refronted houses all over the country. An up-to-date fashionable appearance could be combined with the advantages of new windows (and often the new sashes) and more headroom in the upper storey without too great an out-lay. The new front to a house in Burford can stand for a host of others[57]. It is attributed to Christopher Kempster. Like other craftsmen working for Wren in London he turned architect on occasion, and back in his native town designed this 'modern' house with its parapet replacing the tradi-tional Cotswold gables. Kempster, like the Strongs of Taynton quarries, was recruited by Wren to rebuild St Paul's and the City churches, and it is difficult to overestimate the importance of this training ground for the spread of the classical style outside London. Most of the building in England at this time was carried out by contracting masons and car-penters. They learnt their trade as apprentices, so that practical experi-ence and personal contact with architectural innovation was the general channel of change. Those who worked for Wren and then built indepen-dently in the counties around London were therefore significant in the general acceptance by 1700 of classical forms. But there were other craftsmen who worked in more distant centres, like the Smiths at War-wick, who were also influential in popularising the classical style. In general it is true to say, the smaller the house, the plainer the style, so that the desire for decoration which led in Court circles to the patronage of baroque art had to be satisfied in other ways in humbler homes. On the exterior of houses this might take the form of patterned brickwork, or a decorated hood over the door, or in East Anglia of pargetting the plaster surface. The simplest versions are incised but in the example from

61. Shell porch and pargetting: Newport, Essex

Newport, Essex[61] the decoration is in relief. The panels are filled with swags and foliage and there is, over the wooden shell doorhood, a deeply carved crown (from which the house takes its name). The house, like the one at Burford, was refronted: in this case in 1692, on a timber framed house of *c.* 1600.

The art of building is not just that of architectural style. It is also a matter of the right handling of materials and beyond that of the right relationship of a house or barn or gateway to its surroundings. Vernacular building is determined by local materials and a local tradition, and its designer was usually anonymous. Dating is hard, and it is difficult therefore to describe vernacular building of the 1690s with any certainty. Local traditions of building were still strong in the remoter areas of England (it is impossible to be sure whether some Cumbrian farmhouses were built in the seventeenth, eighteenth or nineteenth centuries without documentary evidence). But even in wealthier counties there is plenty of humbler building that was unaffected by the triumph of the classical style over the town or manor house. The dominant reason is an economic one: the cost of cartage of materials was enormous and local resources had to be used. But, beyond that, function was considered more important than design and since existing forms of building had usually proved satisfactory there was no incentive to change. The lack of professional architects was a further factor for this increased dependence on local craftsmen, skilled in the familiar but not in 'foreign' styles. Moreover, though the local landowner might employ a contracting-mason to design in the latest manner he knew (and that was often old-fashioned) the cottager often built or improved his own home by himself.

Sculpture and Carving

There were considerable opportunities for the sculptor and carver in late seventeenth-century England. Though religious sculpture was nonexistent there was a fair demand for figure-statues, plenty of architectural work and a constant need for church monuments of all kinds. For the carver in wood the fashion for lavish decoration was at its height and the rich woodwork of interiors, whether domestic or ecclesiastical, is a characteristic feature of the period. Grinling Gibbons was the supreme master in wood and some of his finest work was produced in the 1690s. There were others who came very near his achievements but it is Gibbons's style and Gibbons's influence that spread across the country and form a link between a modest chimney-piece, for example, in a provincial house and the superb choir-stalls in St Paul's. Gibbons worked in stone as well as in wood but though his decorative skills as a stone carver are obvious, as a sculptor he was less able, and outstripped by several of his contemporaries. Their achievements cannot be equated with those of the great European sculptors of the day and indeed the average standard of English work was well below that of the continent. A study of the sculpture produced at the end of the seventeenth century reveals that England was not nearly as isolated from the mainstream of European style as she had been and that there are still several surviving pieces that are worth our attention. Above all, the kind of carving and sculpture produced, both sophisticated and popular, can only be understood in relation to the needs and demands of English society of that time.

How did that society regard the men who carved their tombs, made statues of the King and Queen, turned limewood into garlands of fruit and flowers? Were they artists or just craftsmen? It seems that the line between the two is no easier to draw in this area than in painting.

62. Gilded carving on a warship: the stern of a contemporary scale model

Admittedly in sculpture there were those who called themselves statuaries. They were nearly all foreigners and had travelled and studied
on the continent. Like painters from abroad they worked outside the guild

system but do not seem to have aroused the jealousy of the Masons' Company. Perhaps they were too few in number to cause trouble and in any case the guild control was no longer effective. They never undertook building contracts but on the other hand were involved in architectural commissions such as chimney-pieces and exterior carving. The traditional mason–sculptors turned their hands to anything that was wanted and some of them designed and built houses as well as monuments (see p. 142 and [57]). Their contacts with European styles of sculpture were made at secondhand, in England: they were not travellers. Yet the finest bust of the century was sculpted by one of their number who had never been in Europe and whose commitments as a carver and contractor at St Paul's and in much of London's rebuilding kept him from the art at which he excelled. This was the 1673 bust of Wren by Edward Pierce and many of its qualities are also found in the bust of Thomas Evans which he made towards the end of his life[63]. Undoubtedly there was a hierarchy among the sculptors with the statuaries at the top and the small provincial mason at the bottom but the higher prices of the best known London sculptors did not always denote a better product. In the less ambitious monuments or in architectural carving the standard of technique was high in many areas away from London and the baroque idiom was being handled with greater assurance. The well-designed cartouche tablet with its drapery, good lettering and a cherub's head or two is found all over the country by the end of the century. It is very rarely signed and if there were any pattern-books none has survived. It represents the triumph of Gibbons's style of decoration and again we must note the missionary part played by Wren's craftsmen. And what of the wood-carvers? Gibbons himself was pre-eminent among them but he may have owed this in part to his practice as a sculptor (even though some contemporaries recognised his superiority as a carver). Some of the other carvers were men of substance who undertook building contracts as well, but they were all craftsmen and it is significant that there is high quality woodwork of this date which remains anonymous.

The wood-carver's role was fundamentally subservient to that of the architect. The woodwork of church interiors, the carved surround of a picture or carving on furniture depended on the design of the building and the overall plan of the interior. The carver embellished a room: he did not set out to create independent masterpieces (however the twentieth-century art market may regard panels by Gibbons and his contemporaries). The stone-carver and sculptor who worked on the decoration of a building were likewise dependent on the overall designer. It was the architecture which dictated the need for such craftsmanship but of course this did not mean that the carved panels or architectural reliefs could not be individual achievements of great beauty. Certainly the scope which the architectural styles of the 1690s afforded was very wide. The amount of external and internal carving on St Paul's was exceptional but Wren's style, even modified to the requirements and purses of provincial builders, demanded more work from the carver than the austerer style of Palladianism was to do later. The popularity of a particular feature might be mentioned here: the shell porch that appeared at the very end of the seventeenth century on the smallish house in town and country[61]. It might be carved in wood or stone and sometimes the scallop design was replaced with flowers, plants or portrait heads. The fashion for interiors was a riot of carved wood – on walls, round pictures and mirrors and doorways, and on furniture. Moreover, the large amount of building being undertaken in the 1690s all over the country increased the opportunities of employment. There were, too, special openings in London for the wood-carver with the furnishing of many of Wren's City churches and St Paul's. In the shipyards it was a golden decade for the carver and gilder. The rapid growth in shipping, both naval and mercantile, increased jobs for the carver because the great East Indiamen had as much decorative work on their sterns and main cabins as the proudest ship of the line. It was a golden period which did not last. In the next reign there was a determined cut-back in the elaborate decoration of these ships as an economy measure and many carvers were made redundant. The figurehead at the prow did not suffer the same fate but this was carving of a different order. It was carving in the tradition of popular art with its bold, arresting outlines and crude design which suited its purpose and was matched on land by the street figures that advertised a trade or house.

For the sculptor there were other opportunities outside the needs of architecture. There was still some demand for statues. Though most of the statues for the Royal Exchange had been completed before 1688, further ones of William and Mary were commissioned by the City of London. Statues were needed to commemorate benefactors of institutions, like Gibbons's statue of the Duke of Somerset for Trinity College, Cambridge, or that of Sir John Moore at Christ's Hospital. On a humbler level, figures of those helped by such charitable foundations as schools or hospitals were often placed above the entrance, or allegorical figures might adorn a college gateway like the statues of Geometry, Astronomy and others on the gate tower of Trinity College, Oxford. An occasional bust was ordered, perhaps to commemorate the Mastership of a London

63. Edward Pierce: marble bust of Thomas Evans

guild[63], though it was not yet the fashion to adorn a gentleman's library with them. The widest opportunities came, however, in the never-failing demand for tombs and monuments. These must have comprised the bulk of the work done in a mason's yard. They ranged from the large architectural piece to the simple tablet, and in the churchyard from the headstone to the elaborate chest-tomb. They included both the sophisticated and the naive, the fashionable London baroque and the local vernacular. The

149

churchyard was the only place where regional styles in stone-carving still survived and where a genuine folk art in stone decoration could be found to match the popular art of the woodcut.

The influence of the baroque movement in England can be traced much earlier in church monuments than it can be in architecture. Sculpture is art on a smaller scale than architecture and is therefore likely to be more responsive to new ideas. On the other hand the traditional apprentice-trained masons who were responsible for the majority of church monuments had no direct experience of European styles. So the channel of change was the handful of foreign-trained statuaries with the encouragement of their travelled patrons. The new element of dramatic emotion that is the essence of baroque art appeared in some English figure sculpture after the Restoration. More widely, the effigy on a tomb portrayed in death gave way to a figure posed in life. Yet there was no sudden surrender to the new style and it worked its way into English monuments in a more restrained form than that of Bernini, the supreme master of baroque display in Europe. There was a natural resistance to a highly emotional art that was so often expressed in Catholic religious terms, despite a grudging admiration for its technique. More influential were the links of several statuaries of the late seventeenth century with the Low Countries and in particular with the classical-baroque style of the Quellin workshop in Antwerp. This influenced Cibber, Nost and Gibbons and a member of the Quellin family of sculptors actually worked in England during the reign of Charles II in association with Gibbons, and after his death Nost married his widow. Cibber had shown interest in his earlier work in the more dramatic variety of baroque sculpture and Edward Pierce's busts have a liveliness that link him, too, with this strand. His Thomas Evans bust of 1688, already referred to, is an outstanding piece[63]. The slight turn of the head and the deep undercutting of the wig give an alertness of pose that makes other contemporary figures seem lifeless in comparison. Overall, however, the English sculptors and carvers of the 1690s adopted the baroque ideas with reticence; they used the new forms without complete acceptance of their emotional content. The technique of deep undercutting that produced the turning pose and swirling drapery called for skills, moreover, that most mason-sculptors did not have and this factor must have favoured the less extreme style.

In Protestant England there was no possibility of the kind of religious sculpture found in Italy or France. The only ecclesiastical openings in the 1690s, apart from monuments and the carving at St Paul's, were commissions in private chapels such as Chatsworth[15] where the figures on the altar-piece are allegories rather than saints. There could not be a greater contrast in spirit between Cibber's altar-piece for the Protestant Duke of Devonshire and the Gibbons/Quellin altar-piece for James II's Catholic chapel at Whitehall. Both were baroque in that all the arts were subordinate to an all-embracing design but, judging by Evelyn's account, the sculpture and the painting in the Whitehall chapel reinforced the nature of the religious ceremony whereas the Chatsworth figures of Faith and Justice stand aloof from the worshipper. They have dignity but no emotion. Nevertheless as a total art-form the chapel interior is one of the best examples of the decade. On each side of the marble altar-piece the scene is continued in the painting by Laguerre. The stone architectural columns are repeated on the painted walls; two imitation statues appear to be sitting at right angles on the actual altar-piece and the painted figure of a man on the left is stepping on to the stonework. The architectural theme is carried over into the panelling with carved columns that match the lower ones of the altar-piece.

Cibber had made his name with the relief on the Monument to the Fire of London and with the Bedlam Hospital figures of Madness. He had come to England before the Restoration (he was the son of a Danish cabinet-maker) having travelled and studied on the continent. He established a flourishing practice with several assistants (at one time all his assistants were foreigners like himself). It was not surprising that such an established sculptor should have been given commissions at Chatsworth and, under Wren, at Hampton Court and St Paul's.

Cibber's work at St Paul's included the keystones of the arches below the dome and the fine phoenix in the pediment of the south transept which symbolises the rising of the new cathedral out of the ashes of its predecessor[49]. This, like all the external carving, is subordinate to the overall architectural design and serves its purpose perfectly. Being carved within a semi-circular lunette and not spreading into the whole of the pediment, in the more usual fashion of reliefs, it reflects the shape of the portico below and the dome above. Very little of the external decoration of the cathedral uses a specifically religious theme. An exception is Bird's Conversion of St Paul on the west front which was carved in the next reign as were the figures on the parapet. For the rest, apart from the ubiquitous winged cherub – heads, flowers, foliage and fruit make up the forms of decoration and all is of the highest quality. Most of it was carved by the mason-contractors involved, men like Edward Strong, Edward Pierce, Samuel Fulkes and Christopher Kempster, but Gibbons carved many panels and so did Jonathan Maine who was primarily a wood-carver.

At Hampton Court, too, the external carving formed an important part of Wren's design[48]. The Crown, of course, could draw on the finest craftsmen available: other patrons had to be more selective and, as we have seen in Chapter 6, it was a common practice of the time to employ local masons for the bulk of stone-cutting and dressing but to engage men with established reputations for the decorative details. In the case of aristocratic patrons like Nottingham at Burley-on-the-Hill or the Duke of Somerset at Petworth these specialists were London craftsmen and many had trained under Wren. On the more modest house the carved detail was often restricted to the decoration round a doorway or in a central pediment. It might be no more than the arms or crest of the family concerned or a monogram of the builder. The carvers are rarely known. Anonymous too are the small decorative features that appear on buildings of this date such as a finial on a gable, initials in a cartouche, a shell porch or a gatepost with its ball or pineapple or animal. We may not know the name of the carver but we can appreciate the pleasure he must have had in adding an artistic dimension to the functional.

The setting of a large house offered opportunities to the sculptor far beyond the gatepost. The formal gardens of the 1690s were strongly influenced by the example of Versailles in its combination of vistas and statues and particularly in the style of sculpture. Few of the garden ornaments that were made remain today and fewer still in their original settings. The ravages of the English climate and the fashion for natural landscaping are both responsible. At Chatsworth, for example, where Cibber made several pieces of garden sculpture, most of the figures have weathered badly and been moved but his sphinxes are still on the west terrace and some of the figures can now be seen on the bridge. At Melbourne Hall in the same county, however, it is possible to see many of the lead figures by Jan van Nost still in the places where they were first set up. The parterres have gone and the atmosphere is somewhat desolate but the ground pattern remains of long straight vistas with their related statues. Nost came from Flanders and though he worked in marble on tombs he specialised in lead for garden ornaments and became very influential in this field. The Melbourne group includes some delightful cupids and a more elaborate sculpture called the Four Seasons, finely placed at the end of a vista, but one of his most attractive works can be seen at Hampton Court. On each gatepost at the north end of the Broad Walk is a group of boys holding up a basket of fruit[64]. Even where the lead has discoloured this does not detract from the liveliness of the composition and the happy, cheerful pose of the boys.

152

64. Jan van Nost: cast lead figures on gatepost, Hampton Court Palace

Garden figures of the 1690s were usually based on classical mythology and have an impersonal quality that has been increased by age and weathering. Church monuments, on the other hand, are only there because they are commemorating particular individuals. They were also erected to enhance the family of the deceased and in this category the

153

great architectural monuments were paramount. Large and opulent tombs whose purpose was to glorify the wealth and status of the family were no new thing, but they went out of fashion in the middle of the seventeenth century and returned at its close in a new guise that was both sentimental and dramatic. Nost was responsible for several monuments in this heroic baroque style of which the earliest was that of Sir Hugh Wyndham in 1692[65]. This is very large and fills the wall of the small country church of Silton in Dorset with a total disregard for its setting. The figure in judge's robes stands in an easy, dignified pose above two seated weeping women in classical dress. The architectural surround is exuberant with its twisted columns (back in favour and met frequently in monuments and furniture of the period), loops of drapery hanging from the entablature and armorial cartouches above linked by trails of fruit and flowers. Dr Whinney has pointed out that Nost never managed to weld figures and architecture together so that though this work shows competent technique it remains a surround with separate figures and not a unified design. His Digby monument in Sherborne Abbey is similar in having figures within an architectural framework but the latter is less dramatic and the figures far more so than at Silton. Other sculptors who produced elaborate monuments at this time were Gibbons and William Stanton, both of whom had large practices. The Stanton workshop was a family one of the traditional mason-sculptor type and produced whatever a patron required, whether in the old-fashioned style of recumbent effigies like the Shireburn tombs at Mitton, Lancashire, formerly Yorkshire (possibly the final example of the medieval tradition, and splendid too) or in the new baroque pose like the Coventry monument at Elmley Castle, Worcestershire. The Nost monuments at Silton and Sherborne, however, are the best of their kind in this decade.

Twisted columns were popular in the architectural wall tablet though fluted ones are found too. Often there is a scroll pediment and accurate classical mouldings, and the lettering is well designed and cut. All over the country the general standard in the handling of classical details and in the design of lettering had risen by the end of the seventeenth century. It is rare to find an inscription where the space is simply filled up without regard to sense or balance and there are many ledger stones that are a pleasure to look at. (The same visual satisfaction is found in the brass engraved plates that begin to appear about 1700.) A similar standard of competence is found in the other, increasingly popular, type of tablet: the cartouche. Indeed among these are examples of the most sensitive carving to be found anywhere at this time – and yet unsigned. The tablet in

65. Jan van Nost: monument to Sir Hugh Wyndham, Silton, Dorset

Fulbrook church in Oxfordshire, though not in cartouche form, shares
the same idiom[66]. It has beautifully carved cherubs in the manner of
Wren's master-mason, Christopher Kempster, and may indeed be his,
since Fulbrook is only a few miles from Burford. What is significant is
not the discovery of tablets carved by Kempster or Strong or Fulkes but
the widespread adoption of their style (or Wren's style) which the evi-

66. Wall tablet in Fulbrook Church, Oxon.

dence of great numbers of these tablets provides. The later versions in
the next century became stereotyped but those of the late seventeenth
still have the freshness and vigour of a newly-found style.

67. Reeve of Gloucester: wall monument, Avening, Glos.

Some of these wall-tablets were a little more ambitious and two very different examples can illustrate something of the variety to be found on church walls. The first is one of the few monuments by Gibbons in this decade that carries over into stone something of his marvellous skill in wood. It is a boy's head set in a medallion which is surrounded with a wreath of beautifully carved fruit, flowers and palms, and was set up in Conington Church, Cambridgeshire in 1697 to commemorate the great grandson of the founder of the Cotton Library. In the following century this style was to develop into the popular cameo-like profile. Gibbons was superlative master of the naturalistic on a small intimate and intricate scale. He was far less successful when he tried his hand at the monumental. This unpretentious Cotton memorial is altogether delightful. The other example is a vigorous provincial baroque monument by Reeve of Gloucester[67]. It is neither intricate nor elegant but it has a quality of enthusiasm in its roughcast that the urbane monument misses. This particular monument at Avening, Gloucestershire was probably erected in the 1680s (Dorothy Driver, whom it commemorates, died in 1683) but Reeve was working in the 1690s in much the same style. Reeve is a representative of a local school of mason–sculptors who were adopting the idiom of the baroque without its refinements. There were others in regional capitals like York or Norwich, and lesser centres like Coventry, and in the good freestone areas such as the Cotswolds and Northamptonshire. Examples of monuments from London sculptors were to be found in all these areas, too, for the gentry usually patronised the capital's workshops. This practice must have acted as a leaven. The real vernacular styles, however, were to be found in the churchyards.

Different regions developed their own specialities, sometimes in the shape of the tombstone, sometimes in its decoration. Local available stone of course was an influential factor and it is not surprising that the areas of fine building stone such as the Cotswolds should have encouraged the growth of particular styles or that clear lettering should have been a feature of the slate areas. Tombstones are very vulnerable to the weather and also to the tidying habits of successive generations but the seventeenth century seems to have seen the appearance of new types such as the table-tombs of the northern counties and the chest-tombs and bale-tombs of the Cotswolds. There is an elaborate series of ledgers in the West Riding of Yorkshire that begins in the second half of the century with a design derived from Jacobean furniture. There is a group of monuments in the Vale of Belvoir where the influence of the technique of wood-carving has led to the cutting of letters in relief rather than by incision. In this kind of folk-art motives of decoration are borrowed from other arts such as furniture or the flourishes of the penmen[44] and converted into stylised forms. The Vale of Belvoir headstones have angel-heads with triangular wings but the Cotswolds cherubs develop a baroque curve which becomes a stereotype shape in the eighteenth century. In Yorkshire the angels are in the form of sunflowers. Flowers and fruit are popular ornaments, the tulip included, and naturally the symbols of mortality and resurrection are used: the hour-glass, the skull, Father Time with his scythe. Nowhere is the combination of shape and ornament more successful at the end of the seventeenth century than in the lyre-shaped chest-tomb of the Cotswolds. It is a style that is found over the course of a hundred years (roughly mid-seventeenth to mid-eighteenth) but largely restricted to west Gloucestershire (as the bale-tomb is only found in a small area in the eastern Cotswolds). These tombs have ends which project on each side, curving outwards towards the bottom in the shape of a lyre. Sometimes the lyre-shaped end is treated as an inverted Ionic

68. Cotswold chest-tomb, Quenington, Glos. It combines lyre-shaped ends and bale top

capital, sometimes it is carved into acanthus leaves. Both the ends and the sides are decorated in all sorts of ways. There are occasional portrait heads, or shields, there are elaborate wreaths of flowers, draperies with winged cherub-heads and symbols of mortality and eternity. On one tomb at Elmore, Gloucestershire, the lyre-shaped ends are recessed, and standing in one niche is Father Time on a wheel with his scythe in his hand, and in the other a skeleton with his spade and trumpet, no doubt awakening his fellows at the final Judgement day. A few late eighteenth-century tombs are signed but none of the rest can be ascribed to an individual mason. It has been suggested by David Verey that the bale-tombs of the Burford area might have originated in the yard of the Strongs, the famous mason family of Taynton. The tombs of both Valentine Strong (at Fairford) and Christopher Kempster (at Burford) are chest-tombs of this type. The one at Quenington (1697) is unique in combining both lyre end and bale top[68]. The name was traditionally held to represent corded bales of cloth but the more sensible derivation is from the metal hearse which was often laid over a coffin at the funeral. Where there are finials added to the corners of a bale-tomb they look quite like the candle sockets of the hearse.

Grinling Gibbons has been mentioned already but it is now time to look at his achievements as a wood carver in the 1690s. During this decade he was at work in St Paul's, at Trinity College Library in Cambridge, at Hampton Court and at Petworth. He was at the peak of his career and we have superb examples in these buildings from which to illustrate his art. The style of naturalistic carving in the decoration of a room, with loose trails of fruit and flowers above and beside the pictures, was well established before the Revolution; Gibbons had worked at Cassiobury and Windsor in the late 1670s, and his influence became so great that far more work is attributed to him than he could possibly have done himself. There were other craftsmen producing sprays and panels almost of his quality and certainly in his manner: John Selden at Petworth, Samuel Watson at Chatsworth, William Emmett at Chelsea Hospital, Jonathan Maine in St Paul's. There were also several assistants in his own workshop. Yet no one could rival Gibbons's ingenuity in design and his amazing inventiveness. The carved panels on the choir stalls at St Paul's are all different: the cherub-heads are never identical. And the skill with which he could group fruit and foliage and, say, musical instruments, as in the Carved Room at Petworth[69], and yet free them from the wall of which they were a part, was unsurpassed. It is not known where Gibbons trained as a boy but certainly the influence of Dutch naturalist paint-

69. Grinling Gibbons: carving on picture frame, Petworth House

ing of flowers is paramount and it is likely he learnt his art from the Quellins who had done stone carving of a naturalistic kind in the Amsterdam Town Hall. These included festoons of shells, trophies of musical instruments and doves, which all appear later in Gibbons's carving in limewood. This was his favourite wood because it could be deeply laminated; oak which was used in St Paul's limited the depth of undercutting and projection. Yet he did nothing finer than the furnishing of the choir there with the stalls themselves, thrones for Bishop, Dean and Lord Mayor, and the organ-case that originally stood as a screen between nave and chancel and now only partially survives. At Petworth restraint is abandoned. The two double frames (one of which surrounds the portrait of the builder of the house and his wife) are masterpieces. On one the ducal coronets are held up by palms which are so thinly cut that you feel a draught will flutter their leaves. On the other there are putti with trumpets and sheaves of musical instruments, birds and baskets of flowers[69]. Horace Walpole considered these 'the most superb monument of his skill'. Walpole visited Petworth before this room took its present shape by two rooms being thrown into one and therefore before the portrait of Henry VIII was hung over the fireplace. The splendid carved surround to this is not Gibbons's work but that of John Selden. He seems to have worked exclusively at Petworth and other examples of his skill there include the very fine winged cherub-heads in the chapel.

There was plenty of work for the carver while the fashion for elaborate frames remained, and the fashion lasted into the early years of the eighteenth century. There were also special opportunities in the City churches where much of the furnishing was being done in the 1690s. Gibbons himself was only involved in the woodwork of one of the City churches (St Mary Abchurch). The rest, though in the same general style of carving, are by a variety of London joiners and carvers. Very little original woodwork survives. There were again increased opportunities in Oxford where a great deal of building and refurnishing took place at the end of the seventeenth century. Of special note is the chapel screen in University College by Robert Barker, the hall screen in Lincoln College and the total ensemble of the chapel in Trinity. This, like the chapel in Chatsworth, is a complete piece. Apart from the nineteenth-century stained glass everything fits into the overall design: the woodwork of stalls, screen, communion rail and reredos, the stucco ceiling and the paintings by Berchet. There is no documentary evidence that Gibbons worked in Trinity but Celia Fiennes says that the carving is by the same hand as that at Windsor and it is indeed exquisite enough to be his. However, the work of Selden at Petworth shows us that there were other carvers near his calibre and the uncertainty must remain.

A modest house could not boast a Grinling Gibbons but it might have a single carved overmantle and quite likely some furniture in the fashionable manner. Stairs were often a special feature (see, for example, the delicate balusters of the staircase in the Treasurer's House, York) and there were always the doors and doorways. Much of this work was done by local craftsmen whose names we rarely know. Even more likely to be anonymous are the carpenters who erected the roof timbers of a great barn and yet such a satisfying relationship of arch and brace cannot be excluded from the arts of the woodworker (but perhaps should be considered under architecture).

Occasionally we know the name of the man who carved a new Royal Arms for the parish church (a Daniel Earlerman was paid £2 for the one he carved for a church in Salisbury in 1687). These were usually painted and there are traces of colour left on an elm example in Wyverstone church, Suffolk. It has a most satisfying shape though there is nothing specially East Anglian about it. Heraldry, royal and otherwise, did not lend itself to regional styles, partly because the College of Arms still exercised control over armorial designs. Trade and house signs, on the other hand, must have offered more scope for individual treatment[39]. As discussed in chapter 5, very few of these have survived and our knowledge of the kind displayed in the late seventeenth century comes mainly from the London trade cards of the period and early eighteenth-century prints[42]. We have nothing comparable from provincial towns.

A similar need to be instantly recognisable accounts for the bold carving of ships' figureheads and they share something of the crudity of some of the shop or tavern figures. (The figure of Gerard the Giant in the Museum of London has this character.) A figurehead of a Sixth Rate of *c.* 1670 can be seen at Greenwich, and is a very rare survival. It is a lion, which was the standard design for all naval warships beneath First and Second Rates.

The profuse decoration that engulfed these ships of the line has already been referred to. None of these of course survives but there are contemporary scale models (in the National Maritime Museum) that in themselves are examples of the carver's art. Models of this sort were introduced for the benefit of the Lords of the Admiralty who found the shipwrights' models unintelligible. The one illustrated[62] was made in late 1702 or early 1703 (it has Queen Anne's monogram) as a model of a First Rate of ninety-six guns. It shows the highly elaborate carving on the side and stern of the ship. Did Wren and Emmett take the idea of the carved circular windows at Hampton Court from the wreathed ports of these men of war? They were a feature banned after 1703 when carved decoration was restricted to the beak and stern galleries and anything else was only allowed to be painted. The richness of the carving of these ships of the line and also of the great East Indiamen can be well appreciated from the paintings of Isaac Sailmaker and the Van de Veldes at Greenwich.

The delight in lavish carving, as much evident in these ships as in a Gibbons overmantel, naturally extended to furniture. It therefore seems appropriate to include the latter in this chapter. Carving is found on chairs, round mirrors, on the stands of cabinets and tables, on bed testers, on clocks. The walnut chair, illustrated[71], is a typical one of the period,

70 (*below*). Carved walnut settee with original upholstery in cross-stitch embroidery

71 and 72 (*opposite*). Tall carved chair with cane seat and back, *c*. 1690;
chair with cabriole leg and curvilinear back, *c*. 1700.
These show the revolutionary change in chair design at the turn of the century

though more ornate ones were made. The decoration on the arched front stretcher is repeated at the top of the high straight back. The front legs are upright with scroll and baluster design; the seat and back are cane. It is an elegant chair, made for appearance rather than comfort. However, the cane seat was an advance on the plain wooden seat of the 'Cromwellian' chair. Upholstered chairs were more of a luxury but there were plenty of households who could afford them, and rich materials such as Genoa velvet, brocades and embroidered silks were used on the finest chairs of the reign. A luxurious daybed, in its original velvet upholstery and gilt frame, and made about 1695 can be seen in Temple Newsam House, Leeds. The two-place settee[70] is in walnut with its original upholstery in cross-stitch embroidery. It has the fashionable semicircular

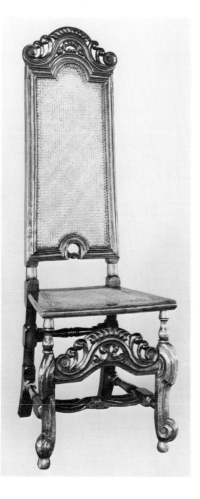

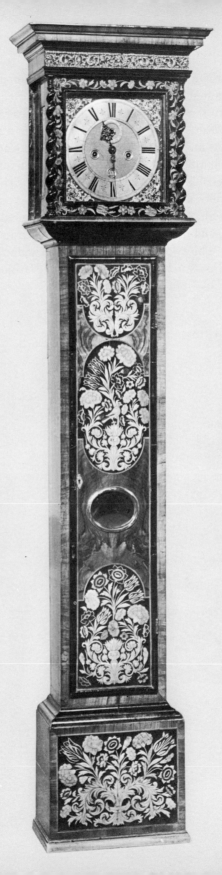

stretcher of the period and fluted legs with square cappings, which are more graceful than the scroll legs in the cane chair, but of course this settee was altogether a much finer and more expensive piece of furniture.

Both the carved cane chair and the upholstered one are types found before 1689 and in basic outline and style there is little difference between those of the latter part of Charles II's reign and those of the 1690s. The japanned cabinet on an open stand[6] remained in fashion, too, and marquetry on all kinds of furniture was as popular as before. The twisted column was used less often on the uprights of a chair but is frequently found on long-case clocks[73] and on table legs. On the surface it seems that there was little new development. Yet by 1700 a chair of revolutionary shape had appeared which led to the great period of English chair design in the early eighteenth century. This was the 'bended-back' chair, shaped in curvilinear form to fit the human back, and using the cabriole leg which did not need the support of stretchers. This substitution of a curved shape for the rectangular panel opened up entirely new possibilities of chair design, only matched, perhaps, by the invention of the tubular frame in modern times. How did it happen?

To a certain extent the cabriole leg was foreshadowed by the scroll leg but in itself this would not have freed the chair from the rigidity of its seventeenth-century construction; nor would the development of the flowing X-shaped stretchers that showed how elegant the uncluttered curve could be. It needed an imaginative leap or else the adoption of the idea from elsewhere. It is possible that the new design was associated with Daniel Marot. He was familiar with the cabriole leg shape in France and was an inventive designer, and a chair with a curvilinear frame from Holland was described as being 'in the style of Daniel Marot'. However, it may have been based on a Chinese chair imported into England by the East India Company, a chair which had a central splat, concave at shoulder level, and a yoke-shaped cresting rail. The chair illustrated[72] dates from about 1700. It combines the two features of cabriole leg and curvilinear back. It is beechwood, japanned in red and gold with a 'Chinese' painting on the back panel. The 'unity of complementary curves', as John Gloag has described the new structure, made any carved decoration superfluous: its graceful appearance depended on line alone. So the reaction against the elaborately carved interiors which was certain to have come eventually was hastened by the sudden arrival of the bended-back chair.

There were one or two other signs that the vogue for exuberant decoration was weakening. The baluster form was ousting the spiral on the

73. Long-case clock with floral marquetry: Daniel Quare (height 208 cm)

74. Gate-legged walnut card table (height 71 cm)

uprights of a chair and neater front legs appeared with square or mush-
room cappings[70]. The elegant baluster leg of the table[74] would be
hard to match. In Court circles Marot's designs did not encourage simplicity but they were more controlled. The influence of his fellow
Huguenots was having the same refining effect on design in other decorative arts such as silversmithing (see p. 174). In marquetry, which
remained very popular, the colours became more subdued and the designs
more delicate. Besides floral marquetry, which continued to be
worked[73], a complicated form of arabesque marquetry developed,
called 'seaweed', and this used only two shades of inlay, a light wood
for the design and a darker one for the background. These subtle shifts

away from more boisterous forms of decoration were indications of change in the future: the general character of William and Mary furniture was still that of bold, lavish display. Naturally this was most apparent in the great houses and palaces of the time and in particular in sumptuous upholstery and the gilt stands of tables and cabinets. The state bed continued to be a focus for conspicuous spending and the examples made at the end of the seventeenth century represent the pinnacle of baroque exuberance. Like the large architectural monuments they were meant to be overpowering.

Change could also be observed in the appearance of more specialised pieces of furniture such as the card table[74] and the bureau with its sloping flap. The latter had a distinct advantage over the old type of writing cabinet with its fall-front let down for writing. There was no need to clear away all the papers before closing and locking: there was now room where they could be left. From this developed the bureau-cabinet which combined a chest, bureau and cabinet in a single piece of furniture, with two slides to support the sloping top of the central portion.

If functional need influenced the kind of piece produced at the top end of the market, it was dominant at the lower end. In country districts furniture was still made by the carpenter and the joiner, though the chair-maker had appeared as a specialist who might adapt features from the fashionable craftsman in town. Spindle-back chairs with rush seats were modified but never submerged by changes in sophisticated fashion; and the Windsor chair, which originated sometime in the second half of the seventeenth century, developed the tradition of stick furniture but was not averse to adopting 'barley-sugar' rails or (in the eighteenth century) a pierced splat or cabriole leg. Like all traditional crafts the exact dating of country furniture is difficult. Names of makers are unknown and changes came slowly. Pieces made on the occasion of a marriage, however, were often dated, and initialled, and many of these chests, cupboards and chairs might have been made by the bridegroom for his new home. They were lovingly ornamented. Folk art carving of this kind has survived reasonably well. It was treasured for its sentimental value, of course, but it could also be an important piece of furniture like the Lake District cupboard that served as a screen in the living room or the kind of press-cupboard represented by the Welsh tridarn. There is an unusual collection of late seventeenth-century oak furniture in the yeoman house of Townend in Troutbeck, Cumbria. Here members of the Browne family (who built the house and lived in it for three hundred years) satisfied their passion for carving wood. The chair-backs and panels on the cup-boards and chests suggest an earlier age but they are the country equivalent of the fashionable delight in carved interiors.

Besides furniture there were many smaller carved articles that come into the category of folk art: boxes, stay-busks, knitting needles, bowls, spoons. Some crude, some intricate, they all exhibit someone's desire to make a decorative object out of a simple useful article. Many of them were love-tokens, like the spoon illustrated[75]. This late seventeenth-

75. Love-spoon, chip-carved, late seventeenth century

century love-spoon from the Pinto Collection in Birmingham is chip-carved with an ingenious set of small loose balls in the lantern on the stem (not visible in the photograph). The heart emblem was, not surprisingly, a common device in these tokens. This love-spoon bears no comparison with the work of the skilled professionals or even the carving by the Browne family at Troutbeck. It is crude and rough. It does, however, represent the kind of decorative art that the 'submerged half' of the population could enjoy.

Decorative Arts

The decorative arts of the period can be studied in a very wide range of objects made for display as well as for use; from the elaborate silver wine-cistern to the simple spoon, from Tijou's wrought-iron screens to the Sussex fireback, from the delftware charger to the chemist's jar and a great variety of other articles in wood, glass, leather and textiles. Furniture and other wooden ware which are certainly decorative have already been discussed in the previous chapter because of the close connection between architectural carving and furniture. Across all the decorative arts there are similarities of style and this should be emphasised before discussing the products in each material. Similar shapes are found in silver and glass and pottery. Similar designs are found engraved on brass, embroidered on textiles and painted on furniture. It would be strange if this were not so. But the working of each material demands different techniques and has a different potential even though the skilful craftsman will sometimes test this to the limit. Hence the paper-like qualities of Gibbons's carving. This was behind the search for new processes in glass, pottery and brass manufacture, and the end of the seventeenth century was a period of intense activity in all these fields. At the same time important changes in style reflected the rapidity with which England was catching up with continental development and standards of craftsmanship, and in one or two areas taking the lead. Progress made in the 1690s laid the foundation for English achievements in the first half of the eighteenth century in silver, glass, decorative ironwork and furniture. In each of these the crucial steps were taken before 1700. Moreover, in the case of clocks the golden age had already arrived and though some eighteenth-century examples equalled those of the late seventeenth century they never surpassed them.

76. Gold-tooling on leather: filigree and floral decoration (20 cm × 13 cm).
The second half of the seventeenth century was the greatest period of English gold-tooling

Silver

There was a great deal of silver plate made in the 1690s. It was also very widely used. Even taverns and public houses used drinking vessels of silver, according to the Grand Jury of Middlesex who in 1695 complained that the practice encouraged burglars and murderers. Two years later an Act of Parliament was passed raising the standard of pure silver in the alloy used by silversmiths in an effort to counter the shortage of silver for currency. The Britannia Standard was compulsory until 1720 and though it made plate more expensive it does not seem to have discouraged its manufacture. It did mean, however, that coin could not now be so easily converted into plate. At the luxury end of the market silver was used for tables, mirror frames, clocks and toilet sets, for ceremonial and presentation pieces such as the great wine-cisterns or corporation maces. On a lower level was a wide range of domestic articles such as tankards, cups, plates, dishes, or pots for serving the fashionable new drinks of tea, coffee and chocolate. There were little boxes for spices or snuff, castors for pepper, cellars for salt (the large ceremonial standing-salt was no longer used, though a late example was actually made in 1698 as a model of the original Eddystone Lighthouse). Communion sets and alms dishes were made for churches and chapels. The fork was coming into common use and silver spoons could be found in quite poor households but were treasured there as special possessions and were not in daily use. There were both plain and highly decorated examples of such household articles as candlesticks or tankards (just as there were plain functional tables and elaborate ornate ones) and this is a reminder that the vast majority of objects classed as products of the decorative arts started their lives as useful articles. The shape came before the decoration and it is in the synthesis of shape and ornament that the most successful pieces excel.

London craftsmen dominated the market. More than nine out of ten of the pieces of silver plate that have survived from this period were made in London. (The system of assaying gold and silver makes it possible to know the date and provenance of plate in a way that is only shared by clocks among the other decorative articles of the time.) Among the silversmiths working in the capital were a group of Huguenot craftsmen from France, driven out by Louis XIV's persecution of the Protestants and his final revocation of the Edict of Nantes. The silversmiths among them came mostly from the towns in the north and west of France and were not particularly notable craftsmen in their own country. Yet in comparison with work of the English silversmiths their standards were higher

and their products in an ornate style appealed to the wealthy. For a time
the Goldsmiths' Company tried to protect the interests of its members
by denying admission to the Company of more than a handful of the
Huguenot competitors. This was no idle gesture. No silver article could
be sold unless it had been assayed and passed by the Goldsmiths' Hall
and only goods of freemen could be assayed. Some Huguenots became
journeymen for English silversmiths; some appear to have had their
pieces assayed with the connivance of freemen. By the beginning of the
next century, however, the hostility of the Goldsmiths' Company had been
overcome and naturalised Huguenots had no difficulty in becoming
members. By then they had achieved a position out of all proportion to
their numbers and a dominant influence on the development of English
silver design. Most of the high-finished ornamental plate was by
Huguenot craftsmen but more significant was their part in the evolution of the 'Queen Anne' style which relied on form and proportion with
a minimum of decoration.

Influence from France had begun to challenge the predominance of
Dutch style in the 1680s. Naturalistic embossing of flowers, fruit and
birds gave way to classical motives; first the acanthus leaf and then the
flute. This latter form of decoration, which is known as the 'William and
Mary' style, was commonly used for drinking vessels and the fluting, either
vertical, oblique or spiral, was topped by a line of punched pattern. The
two-handled cup by John East[77] is a typical example of the style that

77. Silver two-handled cup in William and Mary style: John East (height 10 cm)

174

78. Silver-gilt ewer in Huguenot style: David Willaume (height 21 cm)

remained popular into the early years of the eighteenth century. English silversmiths used fairly thin sheets of silver which were necessary for embossed work, but the embossing itself was a strengthener. French silversmiths, on the other hand, worked on a heavier gauge of metal and decoration took the form of applied relief. This was either cut-card work from a thin sheet of silver or finely cast detail and was always in moderation so that the form of the finished article was never submerged. The harp-shaped handle was a characteristic shape and this added to the sculptural appearance of the applied ornament. A sophisticated example of Huguenot work can be seen in David Willaume's gilt ewer in the Victoria and Albert Museum[78]. The use of the fork made washing at the table unnecessary so this piece must have been made primarily for display. It is only just over twenty centimetres high and the detail of the decoration is therefore exceedingly fine. Willaume, one of the leading Huguenot goldsmiths, used the characteristic helmet form introduced by his compatriots and the ornamental motives are typical of the Huguenot style: the gadrooning on the base, the cast straps reinforcing the cut-card decoration, the pelmet-shaped moulding with the shell ornament, the cabled girdle with the female mask rising just under the lip and the handle cast as a mermaid curving back over the ewer. Some of these features are found in Marot's furniture designs and show how closely related the decorative arts were, particularly in the Court circle where highly ornate French baroque designs were fashionable. Moreover, when Huguenot craftsmen could display such skill on a small piece it was not surprising that English silversmiths complained later (in 1711) that they were 'forced to bestow much more time and labour in working up their plate than hath been the practice in former times'. Their competitors were not merely charging less: they were offering goods of higher quality.

The most elaborate pieces made at this time were the monumental wine-cisterns and monteiths that only the wealthiest individuals or corporate bodies could afford. The Earl of Devonshire paid over £1200 for a wine-cistern in 1687. It weighed nearly three thousand, five hundred ounces (ninety-nine kilogrammes) and would have been used at a banquet to hold and cool the bottles of wine. Illustration 14 shows a fine example (in the Victoria and Albert Museum) with lion heads gripping the handles. It was made by Ralph Leeke. A monteith was a smaller bowl fitted with a detachable scalloped rim on which wine-glasses could be hung upside down and cooled in the water.

Nearly all these pieces of highly ornate plate were made by Huguenot silversmiths, the best of whom included David Willaume, Pierre Harache and Pierre Platel. Inevitably their patronage by the wealthy gave them a leading position among silversmiths in London. More important for the future, however, was the imitation by the English craftsmen of the Huguenot skills in casting and finishing. The Huguenots had brought with them a flair for shape as well as advanced techniques in casting, and together these formed the basis for the 'Queen Anne' style of the early eighteenth century. Of course the demand for plain domestic plate was partly a matter of money; ornamentation could double or treble the price. Moreover, increasing prosperity meant that more households could afford silver instead of pewter on their tables. But this does not account for the predominance of a style which depended on the simplicity of form and proportion alone. Only a shift in fashion can explain that. There is a close parallel here between silver and furniture. The curvilinear chair and the Queen Anne teapot both rely for their beauty on shape and both are the outcome of a reaction against lavish ornament. The coffee-pot by John Chartier (London 1700) has an uncluttered look, with its tapering body and decoration confined to the lid[79]. Even the humble spoon shows

79. Silver coffee-pot: John Chartier (height 21.6 cm)

this transformation. From about 1700 the bowl and stem were forged in one piece and the abrupt junction noticeable in earlier spoons gave way to a more graceful curve. In a similar manner the cabriole leg shed its early angularity for a curve that is taken right into the seat. In this movement towards more graceful form the Huguenot silversmiths played a crucial role.

Decorative Ironwork and Other Metals

Some of the techniques of the silversmith were used on other metals. Occasionally pewter tavern pots were decorated with fluting[77] or with a kind of shallow engraving known as wriggled work, though most were plain utilitarian tankards, in the same shape as silver tankards and showing at the end of the century the same movement towards domed rather than flat-topped lids.

The gunsmith, like the silversmith, could be a very fine engraver. The butt ends of ornate pistols might well be inlaid with silver and their brass or steel parts delicately chiselled (and sometimes inlaid too). A magnificent pair of flintlock pistols in the Tower of London illustrates yet again the debt of English manufactures to Huguenot refugees[80]. They were

80. Pair of flintlock pistols by Pierre Monlong

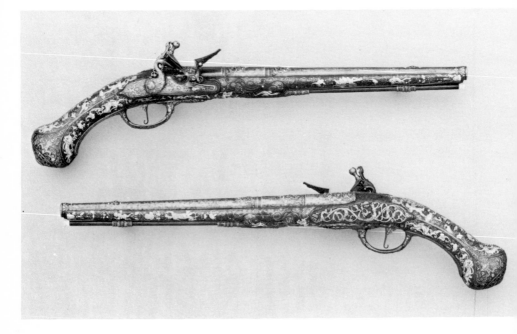

made by Pierre Monlong, almost certainly for William III. Monlong had been a gunmaker to the French royal household before he emigrated to England and became Gentleman Armourer-in-Ordinary to William III. Not only were his weapons, and those of a few other Huguenots, of outstanding quality but they were also to have a great influence on English design.

Brass was widely used in a decorative way, both shaped by hammering and engraved. Until the early years of the eighteenth century and the establishment of brass works in the Bristol region, the only other manufactory of brass was in Surrey, but even so English craftsmen preferred the finer quality of the Dutch product. Not surprisingly Dutch designs were much copied in the second half of the seventeenth century. The chandelier in the Ipswich Meeting-House[17] is in fact Dutch but English ones of this kind were being made. The handsome pair of chandeliers in Cirencester church, for instance, were made in Bristol in 1701 but based on a much earlier Dutch design. Brass can take fine engraving and there were a variety of articles decorated in this way. Memorial brasses have already been mentioned in the previous chapter: here one further example must suffice, that of clocks. By the 1690s the making of a clock involved several specialist craftsmen, such as spring-makers, engravers, gilders and case-makers, but it was the clock-maker who designed the clockwork and the dial and placed his order for the wooden cases. The earlier lantern clocks had been enclosed with brass plates but even after the development of the wooden case for the pendulum and spring clocks there was plenty of decorative work for the metal-worker. The centres of the dials were still sometimes patterned but more often left plain to increase legibility and the corners given decorative mounts, frequently with cherub-heads. The spring clocks retained their brass back plates and these were finely engraved in floral or arabesque designs. The English clocks of the late seventeenth century were unrivalled in Europe. The accuracy of their timekeeping (within about ten seconds a day) and the elegance of the entirely new shape of furniture led to widespread demand in England and abroad. Unlike so many other areas of the decorative arts the leading craftsmen were all English: Thomas Tompion, Joseph Knibb, Daniel Quare[73]. The crucial development in this case was the adoption of the pendulum and the design of the long-case which had taken place a generation earlier; and though the family of Fromanteel, who played a leading part in that, were of Dutch descent, they were well integrated among the London clockmakers and the later inventions and improvements in design were made by Englishmen.

The commonest metal, and one that had been used in a decorative way for centuries, was iron. It was made into locks and keys; gates, railings and weather-vanes; utensils and firebacks. Its craftsmen ranged from local blacksmiths who rarely moved beyond utilitarian jobs to the designers of ornamental gates. Among the latter in the 1690s was a superb artist who brought a new style into English decorative ironwork and, with his disciples, produced some of the finest examples ever made in this country. He was yet another Huguenot, Jean Tijou, who came over to

81. Detail of wrought-iron screen at Hampton Court Palace: Jean Tijou

England with William III. His daughter married the painter, Louis Laguerre, and he lived in England until 1712, but nothing else is known about him except the book of designs which he published in 1693 and the marvellous wrought iron gates that he created in St Paul's and at Hampton Court. He worked elsewhere but so did his pupils and it is impossible to be certain who was responsible. What is undeniable is that Tijou's influence can be recognised in the new use of repoussé.

Hitherto this technique of embossing designs from the back had been used by goldsmiths and silversmiths but never in such a hard metal as iron. Tijou's repoussé work gave a three-dimensional character to his

180

gates. The masks and acanthus leaves, the gargoyles and heraldic emblems appear carved rather than hammered into shape. The remarkable detail that he was able to achieve from a sheet of iron can be seen in illustration 81. This is the top of one of the panels from the Fountain Screen at Hampton Court. It was a royal screen indeed, made, like so much of the decoration at Hampton Court, to glorify the Crown. It was a costly symbol, too: Tijou was paid £2160 2s 0¼d. There are twelve panels, each over three metres high and displaying a different royal emblem at the centre, such as the rose of England, the fleur de lys of France, the harp of Ireland and the interlaced initials of William and Mary. Each is topped by a mask, each differently designed, and superbly executed. The mask and the tassels of the cloth of estate are motives of French design found also in furniture and silver. The design for this screen in Tijou's *New Book of Drawings*[82] is a little denser and more elaborate

82. Jean Tijou: design for part of wrought-iron screen at Hampton Court Palace

than the executed work, and the urns and flowers on top of the pillars were transformed into crowns. Yet the structure of the scrolls, their clothing in acanthus leaves and the main features of mask and emblem are reproduced very closely. Only a very skilled craftsman could attempt anything as complicated as this but ideas could be adapted and simpler examples imitated. The mace-rest in the parish church of Newcastle under Lyme, for instance, had gargoyles just like those of the Fountain Screen. The balusters in the staircase of Trinity College Library by a London smith called Partridge correspond to a design in Tijou's book and, since they were made in 1691–2 and the book not published till 1693, this presupposes some acquaintance with Tijou's work. Partridge's gates beneath the Library do not have Tijou's imaginative flair and the best exponents of the new style were Thomas Robinson, William Edney and Robert Bakewell. Of these we know that Robinson worked with Tijou at St Paul's from 1698 onwards. Edney may have done so, and his work in Bristol in the early years of the eighteenth century shows a close relationship with Tijou's style. The extant examples of these three brilliant artists all lie beyond the dates of this book but together they represent the peak of English achievement in decorative wrought iron. They also show how quickly the new style was adopted and developed by smiths outside London, for Bakewell worked in Derbyshire and Edney in the West Country. The sword-rest[83] by the latter illustrates his decorative work on a much smaller scale than ornamental gates. These sword-rests were commonly erected in churches patronised by city corporations and held the civic sword or mace during the service. Many were more ornate than this one but this includes the characteristic Tijou gargoyle.

Blacksmiths like Edney worked in wrought iron. Cast iron was also used decoratively but only for small items. The most attractive of these were firebacks. The extra heat of coal compared with wood made these protective fireproof sheets necessary in more and more homes during the seventeenth century, and their ornamental possibilities were obvious, and easily obtained by making a wooden stamp that could be pressed into the sand mould. The iron foundry areas in England, including Sussex and Derbyshire, did not produce enough firebacks for the home market, their staple products being ordnance and ammunition, and large numbers were imported from Holland. Dutch patterns were copied by English foundries and attribution is difficult. Designs from classical mythology were popular, and so were biblical subjects and pots of flowers.

Lead was also cast, both for functional and purely ornamental purposes. A characteristic feature of a house built at this time is the decorative treatment of the drainpipes. The pipeheads were often initialled and dated as well, and an elaborate one would have decorative details right down the pipe. Cast lead figures have already been discussed in the section on Nost in the previous chapter (see p. 152 and ill. 64).

Pottery

There were three distinct types of pottery being made in England in the late seventeenth century: lead-glazed earthenware, tin-glazed delftware and a kind of stoneware glazed by throwing salt into the kiln. In each

83. Wrought-iron sword-rest by William Edney

of these there were interesting developments as potters strove to produce something finer that might approach the quality of the imported wares from China. Experiments in making a true hard-paste porcelain were unsuccessful but innovations in stoneware were highly significant. They were the first steps along the path that led to the Wedgwood triumphs of the eighteenth century.

The traditional English earthenware was a coarse red ware, relatively low-fired and lead-glazed, which was made into articles for farm and household use: jugs, pitchers, pots and so forth. It was widely made but already in the seventeenth century Staffordshire had established itself as the home of many independent potters with a reputation for the decorated form of earthenware known as slipware. This was made for special occasions such as christenings or marriages and chiefly consisted of dishes, two-handled cups and posset-pots. As the decoration was applied in the form of coloured clays while they were wet, delicate lines were impossible and indeed the attraction of slipware comes from the bold and robust nature of the designs. It required great skill to achieve figures or the beautiful trailed decoration of tulips or other flowers. Particularly effective was the technique of using a light-coloured slip on a dark ground. A feathered pattern is also a characteristic decoration and was produced by passing a comb or stick backwards and forwards on the fluid slip in a twisting movement. Slipware was made elsewhere in the country (Bristol and Wrotham in Kent, for example), but Staffordshire was by far the most important centre. Ralph Simpson's charger[84] is a splendid example of what a really skilful potter could achieve.

Hard stoneware, which is salt and not lead glazed, was made in the Rhineland and known as Cologne ware when imported into this country. However, the man who appears to have been the first to make it in England did not learn the method abroad but by experimenting with clay in Cheshire. John Dwight was the Registrar and Secretary to the Bishop of Chester but he abandoned his legal career when he secured a patent for his stoneware in 1672. He set up a manufactory in Fulham and besides the brown mugs and bottles[85] which were the mainstay of the business he produced a white translucent stoneware modelled into busts and figures. The quality of the stoneware impressed his contemporaries and the surviving pieces confirm their opinion (especially the touching portrait of Dwight's baby daughter now in the Victoria and Albert Museum). However, it is likely that the Fulham pottery was no longer producing these in the 1690s. The lawsuits which Dwight initiated against several potters who, he said, were infringing his patent were concerned with utili-

84. Slipware dish by Ralph Simpson with portrait of William III.
The trellis pattern on the border is characteristic of Simpson (diameter 43 cm)

85. Stoneware 'Greybeard' bottle, probably Dwight,
decorated with applied male and female heads (height 21 cm)

tarian wares, particularly the 'brown stone mugs'. It is clear that stoneware was now being made in Staffordshire, Nottingham and other Mid-
land towns. James Morley of Nottingham produced a wide variety of
wares including mugs with a pierced decoration. Francis Place, the amateur etcher, was interested in the new technique and experimented with
it in York over a number of years. More significantly, two of Dwight's
competitors were David and John Phillip Elers who were making not only
the brown stoneware mugs but a new kind of unglazed red stoneware.

The Elers brothers were born in the Netherlands and the elder, at least,
had lived in Cologne and learnt the technique of making Cologne ware.
They might have seen or heard about experiments in Holland to imitate
the Chinese red stoneware from Yi-hsing. In any case they were producing fine red teapots themselves in England from about 1690. These were
made from unglazed red clay, rendered non-porous by hard firing instead

of glazing. They were copied in texture, shape and decoration from the imported teapots and were highly regarded by contemporaries. Even though John Houghton's commendation – 'hardly discerned from China, and other Pots from beyond the Sea' – should be taken with a pinch of

86. Unglazed red stoneware teapot (height 11 cm)

salt since he was a dealer in tea, there were other less prejudiced admirers. When Celia Fiennes rode through Staffordshire in 1698 she tried to visit the pottery in Newcastle-under-Lyme to see 'the making of ye fine tea potts, Cups and saucers of y^t wch comes from China'. Many years later Josiah Wedgwood was in no doubt that the innovations of the Elers brothers had been crucial to future developments. They showed the Staffordshire potters how to refine the local red clay so that it could be used for the finest tableware. They introduced the use of a horizontal lathe after the pot had been hardened by drying, so that a smoother finish could be obtained, and they used small metal stamps or seals to produce delicate crisp reliefs of prunus sprays in the Chinese manner. Tea was expensive so the early articles connected with its drinking were on a small scale. The teapot illustrated[86] is only eleven centimetres high and this emphasises the neatness of the ornamentation. It is noteworthy also that the Elers brothers were silversmiths by profession, as were many of the eighteenth-century porcelain-makers. Despite the quality of their wares, the Elers went bankrupt in 1700, but their type of red stoneware continued to be made by other potters (and often wrongly attributed to the Elers).

Chinese influence was felt strongly, too, in delftware, the third type of pottery being made in England. This tin-glazed earthenware with painted decoration had been introduced a century earlier by immigrants from the Low Countries, and potteries were soon firmly established in

87. Delftware posset-pot decorated with chinoiserie designs, Bristol (height 15 cm)

Lambeth and Southwark. By the late seventeenth century there were flourishing potteries in the Bristol area, at Brislington and at Temple Back in the city itself. Though polychrome delftware continued in popularity, the blue and white gained ground, especially in the sophisticated pieces. If delft potters could not discover the secret of the Chinese blue and white porcelain at least they could produce a ware as like it as possible. Some articles like teapots imitated shape as well as colour and decoration.

188

88. Delftware Adam and Eve charger, Brislington (diameter 33 cm)

Others used Chinese patterns or, more usually, a European impression of a Chinese pattern. No English pottery produced anything as magnificent as the urns or flower pyramids which can be seen in Dyrham Park and Hampton Court and were made in Delft itself. These were far removed from Chinese models. Many were designed by Daniel Marot in his baroque style and were avidly bought by Queen Mary and members of the Court circle. Only the privileged few could afford delft of this quality but the fashion was infectious and stimulated the demand for delftware made in this country. Lambeth was able to produce much more sophisticated work than Bristol, including bowls or vases with elaborate scenes of groups of people or birds and plants in the Chinese manner. (Illustration 87 is a Bristol example.) One potter's list of items available in 1696 mentions flower pyramids, punch-bowls and chocolate cups among a large number of wares. The top quality 'fine large rib'd Jars' cost as much as £3 a pair but cheaper ones were only five shillings. Attribution between Lambeth and Bristol is difficult, however, with the blue-dash chargers, which are the large decorative dishes edged with sloping slashes of blue, though the cruder designs are probably Bristol. They usually have a hole in the back of the foot for hanging. These are the show-pieces of traditional English delft. They owe nothing to Chinese influence and nothing to the baroque. Portraits of royalty[13] were popular and often copied or traced from an engraving. Another favourite topic was that of Adam and Eve beneath the apple tree with the serpent coiling round the trunk[88]. The vigour of these designs often compensates for their crudity but perhaps the finest examples of popular art are the Tulip chargers. These, by the end of the seventeenth century, had become a stylised pattern of blue or greenish-blue leaves and orange tulip flowers springing from a vase or mound. A simplified floral design is found on smaller plates or bowls and a cartouche with initials is a favourite decoration for jugs and posset-pots. Delftware like other pottery was made for everyday use as well as for display or special occasions. There were roughly made pots with crude linear decoration. There were more elegant chemist's jars and wine bottles, inscribed with the names of the contents. Many pieces were both useful and decorative like the hand-warmers made in the shape of a cat. Pill slabs with the arms of the Apothecaries' Company were used as advertisements and sometimes a house sign was made as a tile. Purely ornamental pieces were the delftware shoes, some of which have initials and dates and must therefore have been made to mark a particular event or anniversary.

Glass

The invention of lead crystal in the 1670s by George Ravenscroft led to a rapid expansion of the English glass industry and by 1700 English glass was undisputedly the best in Europe. Venetian soda glass which could be worked into elaborate shapes was also fragile and the hope of finding a tougher material was one of the reasons behind Ravenscroft's experiments. At first his glass tended to develop a mass of tiny cracks but the problem of this 'crisselling' was finally overcome by the addition of lead oxide. The flints which gave the glass its original (and still used) name were soon replaced by sand, and Ravenscroft's formula produced a glass which was not only heavier but with a greater brilliance and higher refractive qualities. Here at last was a glass that was strong enough for daily use as well as being an adornment for the table. Soon the new process was being carried out in several London glasshouses and then quickly spread to Bristol, Stourbridge and Newcastle. By the end of the century there were about thirty glasshouses making the new material, though the nine of these in London were the major producers. Demand increased at home and abroad as the cost of the new glass dropped. It is doubtful whether the Excise duty imposed in 1695, and removed in 1699, impeded the sale of lead crystal glassware despite the arguments of petitions to Parliament. The higher cost would not have deterred the wealthy purchaser, judging by his response to the increased price of silver when the Britannia Standard was established.

There were of course other kinds of glass still being made, of which window glass and bottles were the most important. Nearly three million of the latter were said in 1695 to be made annually in England. Most of them were quart wine bottles made of a dark green glass, with a wide bulbous body and tall, tapering neck. Impressed on it was a glass seal with the crest or cypher of the owner or of the tavern and its licensee. Wine was imported in barrels and then decanted into these bottles by the vintners, often in the presence of the buyer to prevent any adulteration. Other attractive shapes are found in apothecaries' bottles, in green or greenish-blue glass. Some of the shaft-and-globe bottles were made in lead crystal and used as decanters (they were also made in silver). Through the seventeenth century glass had increasingly replaced the silver drinking vessel of the wealthy and now it found its way on to the tables of the lesser gentry and the substantial tradesmen of the towns.

Ravenscroft was primarily interested in the chemistry of the glass process: he was not a pioneer in new styles. Yet his lead crystal proved the perfect medium for the baluster form that became the characteristic hallmark of English glass in the early eighteenth century. The true baluster stem was shaped like a pear but it was more usually inverted[89]. It was Venetian in origin and had already appeared on some of the earlier soda glasses but it was adopted by glassmakers in the late 1680s and 1690s for two reasons. Firstly, lead crystal was not as ductile as soda glass and therefore a simpler shape was called for. Secondly, and more importantly, it was part of the general move towards an uncluttered style where beauty comes from shape and not from ornament. The evolution of the bended-back, cabriole chair, the Queen Anne silver coffee-pot and the clarity of Dryden's prose were all aspects of the same shift in fashion. The goblet illustrated[90] shows the elaborate 'façon de Venise' that was gradually

89. Lead crystal goblet, inverted baluster stem (height 21 cm)
90. Goblet in Venetian style with moulded ornament and serpent stem (height 20 cm)

being replaced. The moulding on the bowl and the serpent stem decoration are typical features. The heavy baluster goblet was a statement in the balance of mass as much as a building of Hawksmoor's. This bare simplicity was lost when knops of different shapes were incorporated in the stem but these did not become too complicated before 1700. The knop in fact provided a safer grip on the wine glass whose heavy lead content tended to give it a 'greasy' feel. Lead crystal was used for other articles, too, such as sweetmeat glasses, flasks and jugs, and glass candlesticks for the first time became a practical proposition in the new material.

192

Textiles

The textile arts of the period include the weaving of silk, the production of tapestries, household furnishings and costume, and a wide variety of embroidered work. It is tempting to add the patterned cloth that the Norwich clothiers introduced to imitate the fashionable light cottons imported by the East India Company. These, however, cannot be classed as decorative art in the way that the silk brocades of Spitalfields undoubtedly can. By the end of the century the silk industry was firmly established and, reinforced by Huguenot craftsmen, was beginning to compete seriously with the products of France and Italy. The first notable designs to be woven in England are called 'bizarre' from their jagged abstract shapes, and though the extant pieces and patterns date from Queen Anne's reign they began to be produced at the turn of the century. European in concept, they were influenced by oriental art and were the silk designers' response to the fascination of the East and their rich clients' desire for novelty. Brocades were luxury textiles, used in fashionable costume and in furnishings for the wealthy. Tapestries, likewise, were very expensive. The Mortlake works were only a shadow of their former greatness and came to an end in 1703. Weavers had moved elsewhere and Mortlake's most interesting successor was that known as the Soho workshop in Great Queen Street. There John Vanderbank produced some new chinoiserie designs which were imitations of laquered furniture. Some he made for the Queen's withdrawing room at Kensington though they were described as 'after the Indian manner'. As we shall see, too, in embroidery the influence of the East was the significant new factor in the textile arts of the late seventeenth century.

Richly patterned silks or figured velvets did not need embellishment. They were decorative enough in themselves when used for a man's jacket or the upholstery of a day-bed. Most materials, however, needed the additional art of the needle before they could be described as decorative and this explains why we are mainly concerned in this section with varieties of embroidery. Needlework was a widespread occupation from the Queen downwards. When Celia Fiennes visited Hampton Court she was shown the Queen's closet with its hangings, chairs, stools and screen 'all of satten stitch done in worsteads, beasts, birds, images and fruites all wrought very finely by Queen Mary and her Maids of Honour'. In the Museum of London can be seen a beadwork bag worked by Mary for William III and she was a known enthusiast for the fashionable pastime of knotting. This was the preparation of linen thread in a series of

91. Part of a sampler,
silk and linen on linen
(width 19 cm).
Compare designs with
illustration 92

knots that was then couched onto a ground material in designs that could be quite elaborate. Knotted thread was also used in fringes as on the bag illustrated[94].

Skill with the needle was a prized accomplishment. Evelyn's pride in his daughter Susanna comes out in the entry in his diary in 1693 on the day of her wedding: 'she has a peculiar talent in designe ... and an extraordinary genius for whatever hands can do with a needle.' Girls were taught at school as well as at home and the sampler was the first technical exercise that they completed, often at a very early age. Towards the end of the seventeenth century some samplers became broader and this gave scope for a more decorative composition, with the addition of human figures or a scene, but they were still primarily a tool for practising various techniques. Many of the designs were in fact out of date, for the repeated reissue of books like *The Needle's Excellency* perpetuated earlier patterns[91].

Rigorous training produced accomplished needlewomen and there was increasing opportunity to practise their skills in the home. As the comfort of upholstered furniture became more widely appreciated, embroidered canvas-work began to replace the cane of chairs and day-beds, and a padded winged armchair might be completely covered with embroidery. A much smaller item was the pole-screen which shielded the face from the heat of the fire. On the other hand, the bed continued to offer scope for large-

92. Box with panels of linen embroidered with coloured silks

195

scale embroideries on the hangings and coverlets, and the state bed of a great house of the period has never been outrivalled in the richness of its decoration. Embroidery in the late seventeenth century was increasingly put to practical use but there was still a fair amount of purely decorative work in panel hangings or pictures and the embroidered box continued to be popular[92].

Costume, too, was often embroidered though large surviving pieces from this period are rare. Silk dresses and petticoats, men's waistcoats and coats, accessories such as pockets, scarves and bags were all heavily embroidered. Decorative quilting of both silk and linen became very popular towards the end of the century and was used widely for coverlets as well as clothes. White embroidery was worked on fine muslin aprons and was used as an alternative for lace. Fashionable costume followed French modes and much of it must have been made by professionals. It is not easy to distinguish between the work of the best amateurs and that of professionals, especially in the less elaborate creations. Amateurs, however, often signed and dated their work as Sarah Thurstone did on her coverlet[18], but even in these cases it is possible that professional designs were provided.

Formal designs incorporating lion masks or tassels, or the pelmet motive, reflect marked French influence (and for that reason almost certainly come from a professional workshop). The Melville coverlet[93] of white silk damask and embroidered with red braid couching is a good example of this kind of formal design. It was made for George Melville, who was created an earl in 1690 by William III, and the complete set of bed furniture from which it comes can be seen in the Victoria and Albert Museum. Such designs were totally different from the naturalistic patterns found in canvas-work and contemporary crewelwork. A boldly drawn vase of flowers, for instance, was a popular pattern for a chair seat or back embroidered in coloured wools and silks. Occasionally a pictorial scene was worked using a Biblical or classical story or pastoral subject; these were usually adapted from engravings which might well be a couple of generations old. Flowers, birds and animals were traditional motives, familiar from pattern books and no doubt copied from earlier embroideries, too, and passed on from mother to daughter. Stylised flowers were also popular and a box of 1692 shows a favourite design of the period[92]. Boxes or cabinets were often embroidered by young girls when they had progressed beyond their samplers. By this time, however, the flat panel had replaced the raised stumpwork so much in vogue until the 1680s. Beyond the panels inserted on boxes or screens there were some designed

93. Coverlet of formal design in couched crimson braid on white silk damask,
made for Earl of Melville whose monogram and coronet form central motive

just as pictures, both sophisticated and naive. Other small items for the
domestic embroiderer were costume and household accessories like bags.
The linen bag of 1699[94] is worked in coloured worsted yarn known
as crewel, and domestic embroidery of this kind was widespread.

The technique of crewelwork gained rapidly in popularity in the second
half of the seventeenth century. It was used on a cotton and linen twill
weave which was a much stronger material than linen on its own and
proved excellent for curtains and bedhangings. Nearly all of these
embroidered hangings follow variations of one design: a sinuous branch
or tree with elaborate leaves and rising from a mound of earth and grass.
Often there are animals on the mound and among the leaves there are
oriental flowers and exotic birds with long tails. This charming hybrid

94. Large linen bag embroidered in crewelwork, fringe and tassels of knotted thread
(height 65 cm)

style developed from a complicated interplay of influences from India, China and Europe as trade increased between England and the East. It was not restricted to hangings as the 1699 bag[94] shows with its delightful mixture of oriental and western elements.

The influence of the Orient on English embroidery produced not only this hybrid style of the Tree of Life but also a more obviously Chinese impact in the appearance of chinoiserie designs. Unlike silver, embroidery was not affected till the last decade of the century and the coverlet of 1694[18] is one of the earliest examples that exist. It seems likely that Sarah Thurstone's choice of design arose from a family connection with the East, for the East India Company records show a William Thurstone to have been at Goa in 1638 and Macao in 1644. Her coverlet of satin embroidered in coloured silks and silver thread had several characteristic 'Chinese' motives of pagodas and pavilions, rocks, trees and the curving bridge as the central feature. There is a similar coverlet by Sarah's sister, Mary, in the Fitzwilliam Museum.

Appendix 1: Where to Go

Those wanting to follow up the reading of this book by seeing for themselves would do well to start with local museums and with the relevant volumes of Pevsner's *The Buildings of England* where the introduction will help to isolate the particular period. Small buildings in towns and villages are seldom open to the public but are usually easy to see from outside. What follows here is in no way a comprehensive catalogue. It merely gives some of the more important buildings and gardens of the period which are regularly open to the public, some museums and galleries with collections of particular interest and a few suggestions about churches and their monuments. National Trust properties are marked (N.T.).

MUSIC

Late seventeenth-century instruments can be seen at:

London	Victoria and Albert Museum
	Fenton House, Hampstead (N.T.)
	Horniman Museum
Oxford	Ashmolean Museum

PAINTING AND GRAPHIC ARTS ·

Greater London	Hampton Court (Kneller portraits, Verrio decorative painting)
	National Maritime Museum, Greenwich (Sailmaker and Van de Velde seascapes)
	National Portrait Gallery (Kneller Kit-Kat Club portraits)
Cambridgeshire	Burghley House (Verrio and Laguerre decorative painting)
Derbyshire	Chatsworth House (Laguerre decorative painting)
	Sudbury Hall (N.T.) (Laguerre decorative painting)
Northampton- shire	Boughton House (Chéron decorative painting)
Surrey	Clandon House (N.T.) (Barlow bird paintings)
West Sussex	Petworth House (N.T.) (Dahl portraits, Laguerre decorative painting)

Several country houses open to the public have examples of Kneller and Dahl portraits and topographical views by Sieberechts, Knyff, Kip

ARCHITECTURE

Large Buildings

Greater London	Hampton Court Palace
	Greenwich Hospital (now Naval College)
Derbyshire	Chatsworth House
Gloucestershire	Dyrham Park (N.T.)
Hereford and	
Worcester	Hanbury Hall (N.T.)
Northumberland	Wallington (N.T.)
North Yorkshire	Castle Howard
West Sussex	Petworth House (N.T.)

Smaller Buildings

London	Kensington Palace Orangery
Isle of Wight	Old Town Hall, Newtown (N.T.)
Somerset	Tintinhull House (N.T.)
West Sussex	Uppark (N.T.)
Wiltshire	Mompesson House, Salisbury (N.T.)

Interiors (in addition to those above)

Greater London	Ham House (though a few years earlier has excellent late seventeenth-century work including panelling, overmantels, furnishings)
Cambridge	Trinity College Library
Gloucestershire	Badminton House
Oxford	Trinity College Chapel

Churches

London	St Paul's Cathedral
	Steeples of St Bride, Fleet St
	Christ Church, Newgate St
	St Magnus Martyr, London Bridge
	St Vedast, Foster Lane
Warwickshire	St Mary, Warwick
Wiltshire	All Saints, Farley

Chapels (It is usually necessary to make arrangements to see inside nonconformist chapels.) A few representative examples are:

Cumbria	Friends Meeting-house, Colthouse, near Hawkshead
Gloucestershire	Friends Meeting-house, Nailsworth
Norfolk	Old Meeting, Norwich
Suffolk	Friars St Unitarian, Ipswich
	Walpole

Gardens

Greater London	Hampton Court
Cumbria	Levens Hall
Derbyshire	Melbourne Hall
Gloucestershire	Westbury Court (N.T.)

APPENDIX 1: WHERE TO GO

SCULPTURE AND CARVING

Architectural Stone-carving can be found on many of the buildings mentioned above but especially at St Paul's Cathedral and Hampton Court.

Statues

Cambridge	Trinity College (Duke of Somerset by Gibbons)
Derbyshire	Chatsworth House Chapel (Altar figures by Cibber)

Monuments in Churches

These can be found all over the country; Pevsner volumes are invaluable in locating those of the period. The following are examples mentioned in the text:

Cambridgeshire	Conington (Cotton by Gibbons)
Dorset	Sherborne (Digby by Nost)
	Silton (Wyndham by Nost)
Gloucestershire	Avening (Driver by Reeve)
Hereford and Worcester	Elmley Castle (Coventry by William Stanton)
Lancashire	Mitton (Shireburn by Edward Stanton)
Oxfordshire	Fulbrook (Thorpe – Anon.)

Churchyard Tombs

Cotswold chest-tombs: the bale-topped tombs are in the area of Glos./Oxon. border (e.g. Burford, Fairford, Quenington, Taynton); the lyre-shaped tombs are further west in Gloucestershire (e.g. Elmore, Harescombe, Painswick).

West Yorkshire: table-tombs and ledgers (e.g. Morley, Lightcliffe)

Leicestershire/Nottinghamshire: headstones in Vale of Belvoir area

Woodcarving

Greater London	Hampton Court (Gibbons)
	Museum of London (street figures, house and shop signs)
	National Maritime Museum, Greenwich (ship models and figureheads)
	St Paul's Cathedral (Gibbons, Maine)
Cambridge	Trinity College Library (Gibbons)
Derbyshire	Chatsworth House (Watson)
North Yorkshire	Treasurer's House, York (N.T.)
Oxford	Trinity College Chapel
	University College (Barker)
Suffolk	Wyverstone Church (Royal Arms)
West Midlands	Birmingham Museum and Art Gallery (Pinto Collection of treen)
West Sussex	Petworth House (Gibbons, Selden)

Furniture

Greater London	British Museum (clocks)
	Guildhall (Clockmakers' Company Collection of clocks)
	Ham House
	Hampton Court
	Victoria and Albert Museum

Cumbria	Townend, Troutbeck (N.T.)
Derbyshire	Chatsworth House
Gloucestershire	Dyrham Park (N.T.)
Surrey	Clandon Park (N.T.)
Suffolk	Bury St Edmunds (Gershom-Parkington Collection of clocks)
West Yorkshire	Temple Newsam House, Leeds

DECORATIVE ARTS

For every aspect of the decorative arts the most comprehensive collection is to be found in the Victoria and Albert Museum. Other places are listed under the appropriate heading below:

Silver

London	British Museum
Avon	Holburne of Menstrie Museum, Bath
Oxford	Ashmolean Museum

Several cathedrals now have special displays of ecclesiastical plate on loan from parish churches

Decorative Iron

Greater London	Hampton Court (Tijou)
	St Paul's Cathedral (Tijou)
Avon	Bristol churches: St Mary Redcliffe, St Stephen, Mayor's Chapel (Edney)
Derbyshire	Chatsworth House (Tijou)
	Melbourne Hall (Bakewell)
East Sussex	Hastings Museum (cast-iron firebacks)
	Lewes: Anne of Cleves Museum (cast-iron firebacks)
Kent	Rochester Guildhall (weather-vane)
Oxford	Clarendon Building and New College (Robinson)

Pottery

London	British Museum
Avon	Bristol City Museum and Art Gallery
Cambridge	Fitzwilliam Museum
Oxford	Ashmolean Museum

Glass

London	Museum of London
Avon	Bristol City Museum and Art Gallery
Cambridge	Fitzwilliam Museum
Manchester	City Art Gallery
Merseyside	St Helens, Pilkington Museum
Oxford	Ashmolean Museum

Textiles

Avon	Bath, Museum of Costume
Greater Manchester	Gallery of English Costume, Platt Hall, Rusholme
Merseyside	Port Sunlight, Lady Lever Art Gallery

Appendix 2: Further Reading

The author has attempted to take a unifying look at a very wide field, each part of which has an extensive literature. The following list can do no more than suggest for each area a few books in print or readily available through most libraries. Some of these have detailed bibliographies of their specialisations.

GENERAL

BAXTER, S., *William III*, 1966
CARSWELL, J., *The Descent on England*, 1969
CLARK, G., *The Later Stuarts 1660–1714*, 2nd ed., 1965
DICKSON, P. G. M., *The Financial Revolution in England*, 1967
EVELYN, J., *Diary*, ed. E. S. Beer, 1955
FIENNES, C., *The Journeys of Celia Fiennes*, ed. C. Morris, 1947
HILL, C., *The Century of Revolution 1603–1714*, 1967
HOLMES, G. (ed.), *Britain after the Glorious Revolution*, 1969
HOOK, J., *The Baroque Age in England*, 1976
OGG, D., *England in the Reigns of James II and William III*, 1955, 1969
WHINNEY, M. and MILLAR, O., *English Art 1625–1714*, 1957
VAN DER ZEE, H. and B., *William and Mary*, 1973
Victoria and Albert Museum guides and publications are useful for the specialist topics that follow.

DRAMA AND LITERATURE

The works of the main writers referred to in the text (Addison, Congreve, Defoe, Dryden, Farquhar, Steele, Swift, Vanbrugh) are readily available in modern editions.

AVERY, E. L., LENNEP, W. VAN, and others (eds.), *The London Stage 1600–1800*, vol. 1, *1660–1700*, 1960
NICHOLL, A., *A History of the English Drama*, vol. 1, 4th rev. ed., 1961
ROSENFELD, S., *Strolling Players and Drama in the Provinces 1660–1765*, 1939
SOUTHERN, R., *Changeable Scenery*, 1951
SOUTHERLAND, J., *English Literature of the Late Seventeenth Century*, 1969

APPENDIX 2: FURTHER READING

MUSIC

CHAPPELL, W., *Popular Music of the Olden Time*, (1855) 1965
DEARNLEY, C., *English Church Music 1650–1750*, 1970
HARLEY, J., *Music in Purcell's London: the Social Background*, 1968
MACKERNESS, E. D., *A Social History of Music*, 1964
SHEPARD, L., *The Broadside Ballad*, 1962
SPINK, I., *English Song: Dowland to Purcell*, 1974
WESTRUP, J. (ed.), *New Oxford History of Music*, vol. 5, 1975
ZIMMERMAN, F. B., *Henry Purcell 1659–95*, 1967

PAINTING AND GRAPHIC ARTS

HEAL, A., *The Signboards of Old London Shops*, 1947
CROFT-MURRAY, E., *Decorative Painting in England 1537–1837*, vol. 1, 1962
WATERHOUSE, E., *Painting in Britain 1530–1790*, rev. ed., 1978

ARCHITECTURE

BARLEY, M. W., *The English Farmhouse and Cottage*, 1961
COLVIN, H., *Biographical Dictionary of English Architects 1660–1840*, rev. ed., 1978
DOWNES, K., *English Baroque Architecture*, 1966
DOWNES, K., *Hawksmoor*, 1969
HADFIELD, M., *A History of British Gardening*, 1960
HUSSEY, C., *English Gardens and Landscapes 1700–1750*, 1967
LEES-MILNE, J., *English Country Houses: Baroque 1685–1715*, 1970
PEVSNER, N., *The Buildings of England*, 1958–74
SUMMERSON, J., *Architecture in Britain 1530–1830*, 5th ed., 1969
WHINNEY, M., *Wren*, 1971

Country Life publishes articles on houses and other buildings.

SCULPTURE AND CARVING

BURGESS, F., *English Churchyard Memorials*, 1963
GREEN, D., *Grinling Gibbons*, 1964
GUNNIS, R., *Dictionary of British Sculptors 1660–1851*, 1953
PINTO, E. H., *Treen and Other Wooden Bygones*, 1969
WHINNEY, M., *Sculpture in Britain 1530–1830*, 1964

FURNITURE

BRUTON, E., *The Longcase Clock*, 1964
EDWARDS, R. and RAMSEY, L. G. G., *The Connoisseur's Complete Period Guides: The Stuart Period 1603–1714:* 'Furniture' by R. Fastnedge, 1968
GLOAG, J., *The Englishman's Chair*, 1964
RAMSEY, L. G. G. and COMSTOCK, H., *The Connoisseur's Guide to Antique Furniture:* 'Walnut Furniture' by E. T. Joy, 1969

SYMONDS, R. W., *Furniture Making in Seventeenth and Eighteenth Century England*, 1955

TAIT, H., *Clocks in the British Museum*, 1968

SILVER

HAYWARD, J. F., *Huguenot Silver in England 1688–1727*, 1959

OMAN, C., *English Domestic Silver*, 5th ed., 1962

TAYLOR, G., *Silver*, 1965

IRON

LISTER, R., *Decorative Wrought Ironwork in Great Britain*, 1957, 1970

LISTER, R., *Decorative Cast Ironwork in Great Britain*, 1962

POTTERY

GARNER, F. H., *English Delftware and Pottery*, 3rd ed. rev. by M. Archer, 1972

HONEY, W. B., *English Pottery and Porcelain*, 6th ed. rev. by R. J. Charleston, 1969

RAY, A., *English Delftware Pottery*, 1968

GLASS

BARRINGTON HAYNES, E., *Glass Through the Ages*, 1959

WILKINSON, O. N., *Old Glass*, 1968

TEXTILES

CUNNINGTON, C. W. and P., *Handbook of English Costume in the 17th Century*, 1955

KENDRICK, A. F., *English Needlework*, 2nd ed. rev. by P. Wardle, 1967

IRWIN, J. and BRETT, K. B., *The Origins of Chintz*, 1970

THORNTON, R. K., *Baroque and Rococo Silks*, 1965

List of Illustrations

Acknowledgements

By Gracious Permission of Her Majesty The Queen 35; Avon County Library (Bath Reference Library) 1; The Museum of Costume, Bath 94; Birmingham Museums and Art Gallery 39, 75; Bodleian Library 10, 34, 41, 44, 76; British Library 9, 24, 29, 32, 33, 45, 55, 82; British Museum 3, 4, 8, 19, 20, 21, 23, 25, 26, 38, 40, 42, 60, 79, 85; Richard Butcher 5, 53, 89; Masters and Fellows of Trinity College, Cambridge 27; Country Life 37; Crown Copyright, by permission of HMSO 47, 48, 80; John Ede 12, 17, 22, 43, 46, 54, 56, 57, 59, 61, 64, 66, 67, 68, 77, 81, 83, 88, 94; Guildhall Library 2; Holburne of Menstrie Museum, Bath 73, 77; A. F. Kersting 7, 49; Patsy Lewis 58; Mansell Collection 11; Museum of London 90; National Maritime Museum, London 62; National Monuments Record 15, 50, 51, 52, 64; National Portrait Gallery 16, 28, 31, 36; The National Trust 69; Worshipful Company of Painter-Stainers 63; Rector of Avening Church, Glos. 67; Rector of St Stephen's Church, Bristol 83; Unitarian Church, Friars St, Ipswich 17; Vicar of Fulbrook, Oxon. 66; Crown Copyright. Victoria and Albert Museum 6, 13, 14, 18, 30, 70, 71, 72, 74, 78, 84, 86, 87, 91, 92, 93; Victoria Art Gallery, Bath 88.

Index

References in *italic* indicate plate numbers